Helenus Scott

The Adventures of a Rupee

Helenus Scott

The Adventures of a Rupee

ISBN/EAN: 9783744752381

Printed in Europe, USA, Canada, Australia, Japan

Cover: Foto ©ninafisch / pixelio.de

More available books at **www.hansebooks.com**

THE ADVENTURES OF A RUPEE.

WHEREIN ARE INTERSPERSED

VARIOUS ANECDOTES

ASIATIC AND EUROPEAN.

―――――――― FOR WHO SHALL GO ABOUT
TO COZEN FORTUNE, AND BE HONOURABLE
WITHOUT THE STAMP OF MERIT?
―――――――――――― LET NONE PRESUME
TO WEAR AN UNDESERVED DIGNITY.

Merchant of Venice.

LONDON:
PRINTED FOR J. MURRAY, NO. 32, FLEET-STREET.
M,DCC,LXXXII.

PREFACE.

YE modern writers of novels, who excite silly passions in silly people by wretched language----Ye physicians of the times, who write large volumes to instruct your co-temporaries, without inserting in them a single idea of your own.----Ye theorists (a powerful band!) who corrupt all true philosophy and genuine induction by not attending to the never erring operations of nature with sufficient accuracy; who mistake your own disordered notions for eternal truths; who jumble effects with efficients, and

caufes

causes with their consequences; it is not for you gentlemen to judge of my production.---

-----It is not for you ye men who write tedious poems in harmonious numbers; where the necessities of rhyme obscure every ray of reason; where the beginning and end have no correspondence, and where

where the middle exclaims, I have no connection with either.----Nor is it for you, who, having nothing good or inftructive to lay before the public, publifh infinite quantities of nonfenfe under the dignified name of criticifm, to decide on my deferts.——With fuch men who enjoy the momentary fmiles of an infignificant fame I difclaim all connection;

nection; for their judgment is perverted with weakneſs, avarice, madneſs, or vanity, and to their tribunal, I ſuffer no appeal.---

But I will be judged by you ye modeſt minded of either ſex whether or not your names are already enrolled amongſt the authors of the day---

day—You know that it is a human fault to err, and that the limits of taſte are not preciſely aſcertained—this will make you diffident in deciding on my merit where no palpable error appears; and where I am much to blame, it will make you condemn me without acrimony—By you I will be judged who have natural taſte with acquired knowledge; whoſe

whose commerce with mankind has not destroyed every sense of benevolence for your fellow-creatures, and who rather consider the human mind as composed of frailty and perfection than as a mere collection of enormities.

I PROTEST, (though I do not expect to be believed)—
that

that the following pages in my own opinion are so insignificant that to them I should blush to prefix my name: but I think they may bear rank some among the performances of the same species which every hour engenders—My work is barren of incident, and what incident it has, may not be in its kind of importance; but my aberrations

rations from human nature are neither so frequent nor so great as the insignificant and ignorant imitators of Sterne, and other novelists daily exhibit, in their affected and foolish productions.

CONTENTS.

CHAP. I.

My origin. I am found by an Indian, and melted down into a Rupee p. 1

CHAP. II.

Description of the Fakirs. I travel with them to a subterraneous habitation 9

CHAP. III.

Description of the laws and manners that prevailed in the cavern. I set out with my master to visit Hyder Alli. 19

CHAP. IV.

Character of Hyder Alli. A feast and a stratagem. Hyder becomes my master 29

CHAP. V.

I find that power and happiness are not always companions. Hyder's activity. I get into his seraglio, and see his favourite. 39

CHAP. VI.

History of Miss Melvil.----A father's advice to his son on going to India, I am afraid something unlike every modern one. 47

CHAP. VII.

Miss Melvil's history continued. A strong instance of delicacy in love, and happiness in marriage 61.

CHAP. VIII.

A drawn battle, which ends in what is very extraordinary in our days, a complete victory. A mate of an Indiaman not so extraordinary---a rascal 71

CHAP.

CHAP. IX.

True greatneſs of mind. I go to China, where I ſee an inſtance of juſtice on two aſtronomers. A conſultation of medical gentlemen in Java   85

CHAP. X.

I arrive in England. My maſter ſets out on a viſit to his mother. A converſation without any thing of the bon ton in it   101

CHAP. XI.

The travellers again enter into converſation on the road. They are obliged to part. An inſtance of generoſity 115

CHAP.

CHAP. XII.

Characters on the top of a stage coach. My master arrives in London. A pawn-broker's shop   127

CHAP. XIII.

History of the people I saw in the pawn-broker's shop.   139

CHAP. XIV.

Pawn-broker's shop continued. A lord and a soldier, neither of them uncommon characters   153

CHAP.

CHAP. XV.

History of Flora   167

CHAP. XVI.

The young divine. The nobleman of Venice   185

CHAP. XVII.

History of the nobleman of Venice concluded   199

CHAP. XVIII.

The chimney sweep. I leave the pawn-broker's shop, and am carried by a lover to his mistress. A dissertation on vinegar drinking, as practised by the ladies in town and country　213

CHAP. XIX.

The queen. A lover　225

CHAP. XX.

Military education. A jew an honest man　239

CHAP. XXI.

The little woman in Great-queen street 251

CHAP. XXII.

Alexander, Julius Cæsar, Cato, Cataline, Lord G----- G-----, Venus, and Minerva 260

THE ADVENTURES OF A RUPEE.

CHAP. I.

MY ORIGIN. I AM FOUND BY AN INDIAN, AND MELTED DOWN TO A RUPEE.

THE sun saw me in the mountains of Thibet an ignoble lump of earth. I was then undistinguished from the clods that sur-

surrounded me by the splendour of my appearance, or the ductility of my substance; but I contained within myself the principles of my future form, and certain parts of the rays of light remaining in the cavities of my body, by degrees I assumed colour and other qualities which I had not before. In this situation I remained many centuries, ignorant of the world or its inhabitants. At length I was carried by torrents of rain, which fell on the mountain where I lay, into one of the sources of the Ganges, and at last was left by that river on a bank in the neighbourhood of Benares. I had now for the first time an opportunity of seeing the human form, and I easily discovered its superiority to that of

the

the animals with which I was acquainted. The expression of the operations of the mind in the countenance struck me with wonder, and ignorant of mankind, I imagined that this was a never-failing index of the soul. I was surprised to hear the innocent and learned inhabitants of that country, for such in those days they were, communicate their ideas by sounds. Man thought I within myself, (for though I am not blest with the faculty of speech I have the power of thinking) is the lord of this world. He is superior to all the other animals in the qualities of his mind, which I suppose is perfect; how happy should I esteem myself in being introduced to his acquaintance. I now began to hope that my lustre would one day claim

claim his notice. I courted every sun beam, to attract its colouring and metallic principles, and I succeeded so well in my endeavours to improve myself, that I became gold of the purest kind.

I lay long in this situation unnoticed by men, and despising all connection with the surrounding earths. In this period many changes took place. The happy inhabitants of this country were repeatedly conquered. Knowledge, refinement, and humanity fell before oppression, and I began to suspect, for the first time, that men were less virtuous than they seemed to be.

But I shall now enter upon a more material part of my story, for it gave
birth

birth to my acquaintance with the world, and all the scenes that I at present lay before the public.

I was pleasing myself one day by reflecting the rays of the sun on a flower that had sprung up at my side, when I perceived two men, whom I had often before seen, come towards me; I knew them to be connected by blood and long friendship. As they had so frequently passed before without paying any attention to me, I took little notice of them at present, but continued entertaining myself in the way I have mentioned.—What was my surprize, when one of them, running up, eagerly snatched me from a habitation I had occupied for at least two thousand years. By heaven, he cries, while

while he took me up, it is the pureſt gold! Yes, ſaid his companion, but you muſt acknowledge that it was I who pointed it out to you, and therefore ought to be conſidered as a partner in your good fortune. The firſt denied his inference, though ſeemingly juſt, and blows ſoon ſucceeded to words. An old acquaintance, and the firmeſt ties that friendſhip can form, was diſſolved in an inſtant on my account. I was till this moment ignorant of my own importance amongſt men, and was elated at the diſcovery of my conſequence.

My maſter carried me home in triumph to his houſe, and ſhewed me to his wife and children. They praiſed me for my purity and ſize again and again. Tranſported with
plea-

pleasure and surprise, I could not conceive how I should repay these good people for their attention to me.—But my fortune soon began to change; I was squeezed into a dirty purse, and hid below the earth. Deprived of light and air I bemoaned my situation in this place for several years.—At length my master returns—I am dragged from my subterraneous abode—They apply the strongest force of fire to my body, till every part of my substance assumes a liquid state—I am next poured into a mould, which gave me the roundness and character I still retain.—After I had undergone these changes, they called me RUPEE.—Thus adorned with a name and shape, I acquired a little more confidence, and began my travels as you will find in the following chapter.

B 4   CHAP.

CHAP. II.

DESCRIPTION OF THE FAKIRS. I TRAVEL WITH THEM TO A SUBTERRANEOUS HABITATION.

IT must be observed before we proceed farther, that every piece of gold contains in itself a certain number of spirits, which men have foolishly called qualities. These spirits are known amongst mortals by the names of ductility, malleability,

bility, fufibility, &c. &c. and over
thefe there is a fuperior fpirit, to
which they are all fubordinate.
This fuperior is myfelf, the Author
of this Hiftory.—The Ancients called me Phlogifton; and by fome of
the Moderns, I am named the Principle of Inflammability. But, whatever appellation you give to the
God of Gold, it is certain, that it
is I whom the Perfians formerly
worfhipped, and whom all the nations of the earth at prefent adore.
Without my prefence, gold would
foon be but a vulgar earth; fo that
I never defert that metal, unlefs
driven away by the force of fire,
or fome infernal mixture of a cunning chymift. At other times I inhabit gold, and difpatch my inferiors to execute commiffions, or
gather

gather intelligence as you shall see in good time.

But to return to my story. I passed from my first master into the hand of a Fakir; who, in company with many others of his religious brethren, came to our pleasant village on the Ganges.

These men travel in large troops; and, somewhat like the Monks in Catholic countries, extort charity by a kind of religious robbery. In order to deceive the vulgar into a belief of their being the immediate servants of Heaven, they inflict on themselves the most severe penances; they suffer with patience the most excruciating pains; standing in one posture for days together; inflicting wounds on their own bodies, or exposing themselves naked to the scorching heat of the sun. For these sufferings they pretend, that God, or Brama, admits them to a knowledge of the secrets of nature, and the events of futurity. Thus the credulous are imposed upon, and the Fakirs receive plentiful contributions on all hands, for their information, penance, and religion.

I passed through many adventures with these people, as we travelled along the extensive coast of Coromandel. The name of my master was Jaffier Kan. As he distinguished himself on every occasion by the severity of his devotions, I concluded that Jaffier was one of the best of men. But experience

perience undeceived me; and experience has since assured me, that no garb is more deceitful than the religious one. Jaffier seduced young women under the pretence of curing their souls. Jaffier, when he was consulted about stolen goods, took that opportunity of stealing. Jaffier prayed to Brama, and *preyed* upon his neighbour.

But it would be endless to give a catalogue of his crimes, they were as unbounded as the credulity of the deluded people. I wish, said I, that fortune may some time or other carry me to England; for without doubt, that great East India Company, which can keep black men in such good order at so great a distance, will not be priest-ridden at at home. Jaffier and I, after many months travel, at laſt got into the heart of the Maratta mountains, where, with the other three Fakirs, he had continued to travel for a long time, though we were now in a country where proviſions were ſcarce, and wild beaſts numerous. Towards the end of the twentieth day, our company, conſiſting of three Fakirs and my maſter, ſtopped in a thicket, not far from the Indian village named Chichica. They laid themſelves down on the graſs, and each, according to cuſtom, produced his flaſk of wine. While they were offering up plentiful libations to Bacchus, they entered into a conſultation about the diſpoſal of ſome of their booty. Two of the Fakirs thought it beſt to be honeſt, for the beſt of reaſons, ſelf-intereſt. For, ſaid they, if we do not carry theſe valuable things to the cavern, as we have agreed with our friends, our deceit may be found out, and then no corner of India can protect us from their vengeance. My maſter, and the remaining religious, were of a contrary opinion. They were by this time heated with wine, and the conteſt grew high; they no longer reaſon, but fall to blows, which they juſtly thought, carried more weight along with them. Victory ſoon declared in favour of my maſter and his friend, who, in imitation of experienced warriors, made the beſt uſe of it, for they left both their enemies dead on the ſpot. This is an odd deciſion of fortune, thought

I—I wish all may be for the best, as my master asserts, for the unjust has conquered the just. The remaining Fakir* and my master raked some leaves over the bodies of their friends, and presently afterwards fell a-sleep with a quiet conscience. Towards the middle of the night they awoke, and having deposited the wealth of the deceased in the hollow part of some trees, with the best part of their own effects, they began to climb one of the steepest mountains I had hitherto seen. Sometimes they were obliged to crawl on all fours, not without the greatest danger from the snakes that abound in this country. At other places the trees were lofty, but no where could I perceive any marks of man on them, or on

the

the ground, which in some places was very fertile. We came, at length, in sight of a huge rock, which on all sides I thought impassable. My master and his companion, however, continued to approach it, and at last I could perceive a small cleft, by which they made shift to ascend. In several places of this narrow path, if path it may be called, I thought I could see some appearances of art, for at times it seemed less difficult than it had been made by nature;—at last, with infinite labour we gained the summit, when the evening had just began to spread her dusky wings. This summit was covered with tall trees, whose spreading branches had never been impaired by art. My master, leaving his companion, crept

crept into a kind of brake, and laying himself down by the side of a large stone, he three times repeated some words which I could not understand;. he then rose up, and beat the ground as often with his foot. Some moments after this ceremony, I could distinctly hear a voice answer in the same unknown language. My master then returned to his friend, and both of them clinging round a tree, were let down into a subterraneous retreat, with a portion of the surrounding turf.

CHAP.

CHAP. III.

DESCRIPTION OF THE LAWS AND MANNERS THAT PREVAILED IN THE CAVERN. I SET OUT WITH MY MASTER TO VISIT HYDER ALLI.

I INFORMED my reader of our being carried into a fubterraneous abode, and fhall now proceed to defcribe the people I found there. Night had juft come on as we entered

tered this place, and the terrors inseparable from darkness, disposed me to fear and anxious expectation. We were safely landed in a huge cavern, illuminated on all sides with a number of lamps; in the middle of this was a fire of wood, surrounded with men who were regaling themselves with large potations of wine. These were the servants of Brama, whom all India terms holy.—On our arrival the whole congregation arose, and received us with much ceremony, giving us the appellation of brethren. My master and his friend soon made part of the society, and seating themselves with the rest, I had leisure to form some idea of this odd sort of republic.

The number of persons present might amount to five hundred. They all bore on their faces the marks of dissolute-lives, and on their bodies they wore the scars, as they called them, of devotion. Soon after we came in, they questioned my master. if he had made a successful tour. Pretty successful, said my master, thanks be to Brama. On this he produced a wallet, where he had deposited the things he thought proper to give to the society. He took out his acquisitions, one by one, and as he exhibited them to the company, gave a history of the manner in which they had been acquired.

This

This diamond, said he, I got from the wife of a Rajah in the Decan, for promising to send her soul, as she was on the point of death, to Brama; I suppose she has by this time found her mistake: but, however, Tegbeg take the diamond. For a like reason, I received this silver cup, from an old rake with a worn out conscience: but, Tegbeg take the cup. This ring was stolen by a girl from her father, who had intrusted me to instruct the daughter in the right way; I think I received little enough for laying both her virtue and her conscience a-sleep: Tegbeg take the ring. I received this watch from a dishonourable servant of the honourable East India Company, for frighting an honest man's
wife

wife into a dishonest deed: however, Tegbeg take the watch. In this manner he run over a number of valuable articles in his possession, concluding in the same way, with delivering each of them into the possession of Tegbeg.

TEGBEG KHAWN was, for his years, and the grayness of his locks, the most venerable person in the cavern, and he possessed considerable authority, as I conjectured on my coming in, from seeing him seated on turf raised three steps above the rest. From his youth he had been a member of this society, and had always acquitted himself with remarkable success and honesty towards the commonwealth. In the sixtieth year of his age, they chose

him

him regulator, and even vested in him powers superior to any that his predecessors had enjoyed. He alone determined disputes about private property, he settled every difference that arose by his interference and authority; and, with the assistance of another member, chosen for a certain time by the community, he could even deprive a Fakir of his life. So effectually were his commands enforced, that a man once condemned, could not be safe in the most distant corners of India. All the property of the community was under his care, and this he had deposited in an immense vault, separated from the place of abode by doors, of which he kept the keys. Tegbeg was very talkative, and often interrupted the conversation by

relating

relating the incidents of his own life. His face was jolly and lively in spite of his age, and his being deprived for so many years of the light of the sun; for at this time he was above eighty, and had never seen the day since his regulatorship commenced. He one day admitted my master into the apartment where all the treasure lay. It contained one of the most astonishing collections of precious things that can be imagined; jewels, gold, silver, and the richest stuffs, which the Fakirs had either stolen or received, made up the collection. As avarice has often no end in view, but toils for the meer pleasure of accumulating, so those men, who are worse cloathed than the meanest beggars, seemed to me, to serve no great purpose

by

by what they had thus collected; but, upon a further acquaintance with them, I found they had not so far mistaken the art of living well, as I had conceived. They were here quite separated from the world, and uncontrouled by its laws. They had plenty of all the necessaries and luxuries of life, which their cunning could generally supply, or their wealth at any rate purchase. A certain number of them, dispersed thro' every part of India, provided for the rest, who were indulging themselves in their retreat at ease, and these again took their turn of going into the world. During the several weeks that my master spent in the cavern, every day new luxuries were introduced to please the palate, and also the other senses; and every

night

night was concluded with wine and ſtory-telling.—Theſe were the only ſervants of heaven I had yet viſited. I wonder, ſaid I, if all the ſervants of heaven like to live well; do they conſider the joys of this life as the beſt earneſt of future happineſs? It is ſurely not ſo in England, where men, I have been told, are acquainted with the true religion.

In the midſt of theſe pleaſures, two Fakirs arrived with the news that the illuſtrious Hyder Alli had given a general invitation to their body, to dine with him on a certain day. The hope of gain prompted ſome to attend, vanity not a few, and curioſity many. Amongſt the reſt, my maſter reſolved to attend; he sewed me up in the lining of his ragged covering, and in company with about four hundred Fakirs, we set out to be present at the feast given to our body by Hyder Alli.

CHAP

CHAP. IV.

CHARACTER OF HYDER ALLI. A FEAST AND A STRATAGEM. HYDER BECOMES MY MASTER.

HYDER at this time was engaged in several wars, in the course of which, he gave many proofs of great generalship and force of mind.

HE could well counterfeit any character, which it was for his interest

tereſt to aſſume. The ill qualities of the human mind, which afford the the beſt handle for governing mankind, he could uſe to much advantage.—War is conducted on different principles in the eaſt, from thoſe by which it is regulated in Europe. If a general, who is dreaded by an enemy, can be carried off by any piece of treachery, it is looked upon as fair as any ſtratagem in the field.—Hyder was well verſed in buſineſs of this nature.—He was alſo ſkilled in the art of negociation, and could look with great ſagacity into the events of futurity.

My maſter and his companions had heard much of this warriour, whoſe fame ſpread over all Indoſtan. They were dazzled with the honour

nour of an invitation from so celebrated a man, and assembled in hundreds from every quarter.

When we arrived, this great general was reviewing his troops.—They occupied a large extent of country, on which he made them perform a variety of manœuvres. No European can have an idea of the beauty of an entertainment of this nature in the east. Sometimes they would advance slowly in a compact and deep arrangement—Sometimes with rapidity they would run to the charge, every face expressive of the fury of battle, and every man animated, as if on himself the whole fate of the day depended. It was in this manner the Greeks and the Romans fought, when their weapons, and consequently

quently military constitution, was favourable to courage. Now Hyder would shape them into crescents, now into squares. I, who had never seen such a sight before, was in perfect amazement, that one small animal, with such perfect ease could regulate such a mass of motion.

It has been asserted, that the blacks are incapable of discipline; but what may be effected in this way by proper care, a major in the company's service, and the enemy of Hyder, not long ago demonstrated. The Indian saw the advantage of it, from the many defeats he suffered, and with care imitated the example.

The time at length arrived for
the

the celebration of our feast—To the number of twelve thousand the Fakirs sit down at table—Dishes succeed dishes, and dainty dainty; for this was a day, on which, by the express command of Hyder, they were to relax of their ordinary severity. —Good humour and self importance shewed themselves over all the tattered assembly, which, to a distant spectator, must have appeared not unlike a London rag fair—The intoxication of honour and good cheer was universal, when Hyder makes his appearance—The majesty of his countenance, in spite of the smile that then adorned it, struck terror into the congregation—Silence and dread were universal—The animating principle of a whole camp, which extended to the boundaries of our vision, stood before us. After looking up three times to heaven, in adoration of the great Brama, he thus broke silence.

"Illustrious servants of the
" power whom we adore. I come
" to return you my thanks for
" the honour you have done me in
" accepting my invitation. I enter-
" tain the highest veneration for the
" sanctity of your lives, and the se-
" verity of your manners. You
" have shewn yourselves worthy of
" that master you all worship, by
" dispising all sensual comforts.
" You have even gone farther: as
" if you possessed a mind in a state
" of perfect separation from body,
" you have continually inflicted on
" yourselves the most excruciating
tor-

" tortures, and thefe you have born
" without teftifying any fenfe of
" pain. You have rolled naked in
" the dirt, while the rude pebbles
" deprived you of the fmall frag-
" ments of fkin your other fufferings
" had left behind. Illuftrious fer-
" vants of Brama, who fee the chain
" of future events, Hyder Alli
" pities your fufferings.—Be not feen
" amongft men any more in the
" mean drefs in which you now
" appear. Lay afide thefe rags that
" ill befit the minifters of heaven;
" Drefs is a mark of diftinction; and
" you who hold the firft rank
" amongft men, fhould not alone be
" diftinuifhed by filth. I have pre-
" pared cloaths that will defend you
" both from the cold and the heat,
" for well I know you have no
                            " money.

"money to purchase any for your-
"selves. My soldiers shall see the
"servants of Brama immediately
"dressed in them. Such is the
"council that Brama puts into the
"heart of Hyder Alli—Can I say
"more?"

AFTER this speech, he immmediately went out. The whole assembly sat in silent vexation; for every individual was sensible, that his rags which seemed so worthless, contained great treasures. But it would have been in vain to remonstrate. Hyder's soldiers perform with alacrity the charitable office of cloathing the naked, and took possession of the rags, which were heavy with gold, under the pretence of burying them; for what could be
supposed

supposed of value in the tattered coverings of poor men that practised self denial! The operations of war which Hyder carried on at this time against the British, began to be languid for want of money; he saw the evil, and took this method of of providing against it. Thus I escaped, with many thousands of the same species, and found myself in the possession of the great Hyder Alli.

CHAP.

CHAP. V.

I FIND THAT POWER AND HAPPINESS ARE NOT ALWAYS COMPANIONS.----HYDER'S ACTIVITY.--I GET INTO HIS SERAGLIO AND SEE HIS FAVOURITE.

MY new master was of a very different complexion from my former; he was as far raised above the last in real merit, as fortune had placed him in station. I now expected, as I was with one of the rulers of the

the earth, to meet with nothing but a fucceffion of pleafures and happinefs, uninterrupted by care. But time difcovered my error: I found that the moft exalted ftation has its difquietudes, and I foon formed an opinion, which experience has fince confirmed, that heaven has attached conveniencies and inconveniencies to every fituation in life, by which the diftribution of happinefs is more equal than we imagine. When I therefore fee great men in purfuit of titles and power, I look on them as great boys, who follow a foot ball with eagernefs, though they have no purpofe that can be anfwered by fuch painful or uneafy exertions.

But to return to my mafter. At this time a war with the Britifh employed

ployed all his attention. I, who was witnefs to the emotions of his mind, can only have an idea of a commander's life, who, placed in the higheft fituation, has every thing depending on himfelf. Sometimes, like a wretch in the middle of an ocean, he fees no twig to keep him from deftruction. If the officer executes the commands of his general, it is all *his* care—The foldier, with his companion can alleviate the hardfhips of a march; or in the moment of battle, the expectation of mutual affiftance will excite his courage: but a man, placed in the fituation of my mafter, has no fuch comforts as thefe. It is he that is to find out expedients; it is he that is is to remove difficulties. A thoufand circumftances are to be attended

tended to whilft like other men his judgment may be blinded by fear or hope and he has nothing beyond it to rely on. What vigour of mind, and what determined courage fhould a general poffefs! Hyder was conftantly in motion. He flept little, and that at no regular hours. He was himfelf in every place, and faw not only the moft important, but the meaneft duties performed. In compliance with the practice of the country, many of the women of Hyder's feraglio attended the camp in feparate tents. I often went with him to thefe abodes facred to Venus, and had occafion to be an eye witnefs to fcenes, which in this country are but little known.—I fhall however beg leave to refer my reader to the Perfian letters of the
cele-

celebrated Montesquieu, for some idea of a seraglio.

Happy women of England, whom custom and religion have made the equals of men! You little know the wishes of the heart without the hope of gratifying them. You are not placed under the dominion of tyrants, who possess nothing in common with men but the figure. The little impulses which nature dictates, the gentle desires which a new object may excite, are no crimes in you!

The chief favourite of my master, whom he went to visit as often as the cares of his office would admit, may well be reckoned an instance of the wantoness of fortune. I shall never forget the situation I found her

her in the firſt time I ſaw her. Her head was a little reclined towards her ſhoulder.—Her motionleſs eye was fixed on no particular object. I could perceive the big tear ſteal down her cheek, of the beauty of which, no words can convey an idea. She did not perceive my maſter on his entering her apartment.—The generous warrior ſeemed to feel more than all her ſorrows, and ſtood looking at her in ſilent admiration. I had then a full ſight of her charms, which were heightened by unaffected ſorrow; at leaſt her agitation of mind made me admire her the more.—She was rather under the common ſize.—Her face was ſtrongly expreſſive of the ſweetneſs of her temper, and the elevation of her mind. Her form was delicate, and
ſeemed

seemed a fit habitation of the purest soul, for no exuberance of parts created any wanton desires. After continuing some time in this attitude, she began to sing in a low voice. I shall never forget the words or the air, which at that time made such an impression upon me. It was a song well known in the north by the name of the Broom of the Cowden knows. She had just finished the first verse,

  Oh the broom, the bonny bonny broom,
    The broom of the Cowden knows;
  I wish I was with my dear swain,
    With his pipe and my ewes,

when she perceived my master. He advanced towards her with great respect: I come, says he, adorable maid,

maid to hear the history of your sufferings, which you have promised to relate to me. My generous lord, she replied, it will give me pleasure to testify in any way my gratitude for obligations which I can never repay. The story of my life has nothing in it but a few misfortunes that are unworthy of your attention; but as you desire me, I shall tell every circumstance, with as much truth as I am able. Hyder placed himself on a carpet at her feet, and with down cast eyes, she began as in the next chapter.

CHAP.

CHAP. VI.

HISTORY OF MISS MELVIL. A FATHER'S ADVICE TO HIS SON ON GOING TO INDIA, I AM AFRAID, SOMEWHAT UNLIKE THAT OF EVERY MODERN ONE.

I WAS born, illustrious Hyder, in that part of the island of Great Britain called Scotland, not far from the peaceable borders of the Tweed. My father, whose name was

was Melvil, poffeffed a fmall eftate, which had been in his family for many generations. He, like his prudent anceftors, was convinced that a little is enough in the hands of frugality, and he neither wanted to encreafe nor diminifh the fortune he had received from them. My mother was nearly his equal in birth, and they both poffeffed, in a great degree the fame turn of mind. He, with a great deal more knowledge of letters, poffeffed lefs with refpect to the world. I could dwell with pleafure on the virtues that diftinguifhed him above all mankind. The rude inhabitants of the neighbourhood confidered him as their father; he was the umpire in all their difputes, for they knew nothing

of

of a greater man, and they could not of a better.

I HAD only one brother, who was several years older than myself, for whom I possessed the warmest affection, and who returned it as tenderly as I could have wished. We spent the first part of our lives together in that friendship, which of all others, is the most disinterested, and of the purest nature. He was my companion and protector in our walks in the field;—I was his confident and counsellor in all his little affairs, and his nurse in distress. No one who has not had a brother like mine, can conceive my happiness. Our connection was the just medium betwixt love and friendship, for it wanted the imperfections

tions of both. But early in life, he gave marks of a difpofition very unlike that of his peaceable father; for though his natural good fenfe kept his ambition within bounds, yet it difcovered itfelf on every occafion.

At length, he wifhed much to enter into the military line, and only begged my father to advance him as much money as might enable him to begin the world in that character; the remainder of his fortune, he defired might be left to me. This refolution of my brother, was a fevere ftroke to us all, and I believe haftened the progrefs of the difeafe with which my mother was afflicted, for her death

at

at this time, began the misfortunes of our family.

IN reverence for my father's sorrow, my brother seemed at length to relinquish his scheme; but his ambitious mind only concealed it for a time, to prosecute it with the greater ardour in future.

AT this period, my brother had an intimate acquaintance, the son of a widow lady, who had an estate where she sometimes resided, contiguous to my father's. Neighbourhood introduced some connection betwixt our families, and thus Capt. H. became a friend to my brother, and a lover to me.——— (Here the lovely Miss Melvil, in spite of every effort, fell into the utmoſt agitation of mind, which my maſter, with much ſympathy, endeavoured to compoſe; after ſome time ſhe went on as follows):

Excuse me great Hyder, excuſe a wretched female, who poſſeſſes your feelings, without your fortitude to ſupport them. At this period all my misfortunes commenced, for Captain H. was not long indifferent to me. His attention to pleaſe, his appearance, and above all, a mind like his, might have won a heart better acquainted with the world than mine. He ſaw the progreſs he had made in my affections, nor did I wiſh to conceal it from him. As his addreſſes were carried on with the

utmoſt

utmoſt honour, I thought he deſerved my confidence in return.

In the bliſs of this pleaſing connection, a whole ſummer paſſed away, uninterrupted by any care, but the fear of a change. But this was not to laſt long. One day, on coming into the parlour, I found him with my father. Sorrow was ſtrongly painted in his face, and ſilence prevailed for ſome time on my entering the room. For my own part, I was ſo confounded at what I beheld, that I attempted to ſpeak in vain. My father at laſt addreſſing me, Maria, ſays he, Captain H. is obliged, for ſome little time, to leave us. I heard no more, but fell lifeleſs on the floor. When I recovered my senses, I found the Captain still beside me. Maria, he, we only part for a little time, to meet again with more pleasure; such is the will of my sovereign, and the call of my country. Our regiment is ordered to the East Indies, and both my duty and my honour oblige me to attend it. I was struck dumb with this information, and thought my misery complete. How can you think of leaving me at such a distance, I exclaimed, time will have worn me to a wretch, before you can measure back those seas that will soon divide us. But we parted at length, my trembling eyes followed him as he went, as far as distance, and my tears would allow. All the efforts of my poor father

to

to alleviate my sufferings, were in vain. It was to little purpose that he told me, over and over again, the promises the Captain had made; that we only parted for a little time, to meet again with greater joy. By degrees, a settled melancholy took possession of my mind, which the recollection of my past happiness would sometimes heighten into more violent emotions. I little imagined that this was but an introduction to other evils!

My brother, as he found his father so averse to his entering into the army, had applied, without informing any person, to a friend, by whose interest he was put on the military establishment of the

East India Company. This I thought was the last wound I could receive from fortune. My father used every argument that he could think of to dissuade him. He even interposed his parental authority, and tried to take hold of the feelings of his son, as he could not convince his judgment. But every thing was without effect. Preparations were therefore made for his voyage; for, as my father could not alter the resolutions of his son, he resolved to assist him, as much as lay in his power. The dreadful day of his departure arrived, when the misery of my own heart seemed to give a melancholy air to all nature. My father could afford me little assistance under such a load of sorrow,

row, for it was already too heavy for his affection, and his age.—Juſt before my brother bade us farewel, he addreſſed him as follows.

"My ſon, you now go to a
"land, where, of all others, your
"good qualities may be of moſt
"uſe, and where your bad will
"have the moſt room to do miſ-
"chief. The laws, at ſuch a diſ-
"tance from the fountain of go-
"vernment, cannot be ſuppoſed to
"be executed with ſuch regulari-
"ty as in this country. However
"pure the conſtitution may be,
"the executive parts muſt often
"be truſted to intereſted indivi-
"duals, who are little ſubject to
"the detection or controul of a
"ſupe-

"superior power. Let this con-
"sideration stimulate you to a
"nicer scrutiny into your own
"conduct. The approbation of
"a mind that has done its duty
"will be yours, if not the re-
"wards of a generous company.
"I believe you will never make
"the mere circumstance of co-
"lour, a reason for treating any
"of your fellow creatures with
"injustice, or with rigour. Let
"philosophers determine, in their
"speculations, whether or not
"they are inferior to us in the
"powers of the mind. If they
"are so let us never take the ad-
"vantages that our superior abi-
"lities may give; but let us be-
"have in their country, like a
"man, who on a visit to his
"neigh-

" neighbour, treats him with re-
" spect, and ever mindful that he
" himself is but a stranger, allows
" him the superiority in his own
" house.

" Your particular province is
" to protect the trade of your
" country, against the insults of
" European powers, or of the In-
" dian nations, who ignorant of
" the blessings that commerce
" diffuses, even to themselves,
" are often disposed to interrupt
" its equitable course. The prof-
" perity therefore of trade, is
" what you are to have in view,
" not the extension of settlement,
" and much less your private ad-
" advantage. Your profits will
" be sufficient for your wants,

" and

"and if your good behaviour al-
"lows you to advance to a high
"rank, they may even enable you
"to return to your own country
"with honourable wealth. In
"this station in India, my son,
"you may enjoy the glorious ho-
"nour of rectifying particular a-
"buses, you may be blessed by
"those nations, that have so often
"cursed our rapacity, and the
"heart of your old father may
"beat high with the idea of hav-
"ing given life to a benefactor of
"mankind."

CHAP.

CHAP. VII.

MISS MELVIL'S HISTORY CONTINUED. A STRONG INSTANCE OF DELICACY IN LOVE AND HAPPINESS IN MARRIAGE.

IT is nedlefs to tell you, illuſrious Hyder, of my feelings at the departure of an only brother, whom I loved ſo tenderly. My poor father was inconſolable, and all his philoſophy, of which he had

had a confiderable fhare, could not defend him againft the ftroke. Old age had already began his approaches, and forrow completed the work. Without a mother, and now without a brother, I faw my remaining parent laid in the grave. I could no longer remain in a place which my deareft friends had once inhabited, but accepted the invitation of an aunt who lived in a city not far diftant.

This lady, whofe name was Roberts, was of a very peculiar character. In an advanced age, when the world had doomed her to perpetual virginity, fhe was lucky enough to get married to her prefent hufband, who had made fome fortune as commander of a veffel in
the

the West India trade. Her strongest feeling was jealousy, which manifested itself in ways that seemed very inconsistent with her natural good sense. No lady could come near her house, and I was perfectly debarred of every intercourse with my own sex, for I could use no freedom with my aunt, whose masculine manners were so unlike my own. She was not only jealous of the old gouty captain, who certainly gave her no more reason than any other piece of furniture in the house, but of every man with every woman. To such a pitch had long maidenhood and now the want of children wrought up the rank feeds of that disposition in her mind.

WHAT

What aggravated my sufferings, was the crowd of gentlemen, who visited constantly at our house, and whose society alone was pleasing to my aunt. Amongst our visitants, I had many admirers, who were frequently teasing me with their addresses. If my aunt discovered any thing of this kind, it fired her jealous disposition, which broke out in making us all unhappy. My uncle was a good natured man, but he knew very well her unlimited dominion, and never ventured to oppose it. But what at this time chiefly aggravated the uneasiness of my situation, was the addresses of a disagreeable old wretch, who had nothing besides a good estate to recommend him. I knew well that he was a great favourite of my aunt,

aunt, from his infinuating on all occafions, that fhe was an excellent cook, and a well dreffed woman; but I never fufpected that he had any pretenfions to me, till all the country talked of our marriage. Good God thought I, how can that report have arifen; this man, though he poffeffed all the earth, would be the laft object of my choice. But he informs every one that I am to marry him;—furely "I have fome title to be informed " of the grounds of his expecta- " tion."—But I did not remain long in this ftate of wonder, for I found that I was obliged to my aunt for the report. We had juft finifhed dinner one day, when my lover came in intoxicated with liquor, and bedaubed with fnuff as ufual.

ufual.—The fubject of matrimony was foon introduced. "I cannot imagine" faid he, "how all the young ladies are to find hufbands in thefe times, when war and difeafe deftroy or mutilate half the young fellows. It is unfafhionable mifs," addreffing me, and viewing himfelf as low as the foot, "it is unfafhionable to carry found limbs in this world." "Yes;" replied my aunt, "few are fo lucky as you in many particulars, and as to what you well obferve of young girls, they cannot expect offers every day, and therefore fhould make the beft of fuch as God may fend them". "Matrimony," anfwered my uncle, planting his gouty feet with more firmnefs than ufual on the ground,

ground, "is a dangerous bufinefs, "for my wife will have every thing "her own way". My uncle often made this obfervation with a fneer, that gave every one to know he meant the very contrary of his words, and my aunt, as ufual, obferved, when fhe had a point to carry, "yes, yes, deary, you will find "it a hard matter to make any body "believe that you can be ruled, "when all the world are convinced "of the contrary". My uncle looked big, as he always did, at this fpeech, and went out of the room, calling for his beft hat and red waiftcoat with broad lace. My aunt followed him, and I found myfelf alone with my amiable lover.

He

He firſt addreſſed me with all the ridiculous extravagance of a young coxcomb, ſpoke of being entranced, and compared me to a ſtar, which ſpreads an intoxicating influence. Without giving me time to make any anſwer, he propoſed marriage, and aſſured me, that in order to ſave the bluſh of my conſenting, he had already ſettled the articles with my aunt; for your part ſays he, you have only to name the happy day, my little angel. Indignation at this unworthy treatment made me forget all reſpect for my aunt, which was heightened by the reflection that I had no other friend to rely on. I ran into the room where ſhe was, and upbraided her in the ſtrongeſt terms before my uncle, for taking ſo baſe an advantage

vantage of my helpless condition. By this step I had the satisfaction to see my lover discouraged from any farther attempt, but I never could again get into the good graces of my aunt, who, indeed, was much alienated from me before, as the gentlemen allowed me to be a woman by their attentions to me, though at home I seldom got any other title from her than *the child*.

MULTIPLIED indignities at length determined me immediately to accept the offer of Captain H——, from whom I had received many letters, during the three years of his absence. He had been very successful in the service, and as there was little probability of his

his being able to return for some time, he wrote me the most pressing letters to come to India. This was enforced by my brother and some other relations, who at that time were in considerable stations at Madrass. I had so little reason to call his honourable intentions in question, and felt my passion for him so strong, and the desire of seeing my brother so great, that I resolved to comply.—At this moment the noise of warlike instruments, and the firing of artillery interrupted the narration of the fair Miss Melvill;—my master, without shewing any symptom of fear or surprise, desired her to be composed, and then ran out to know the reason of the alarm.

CHAP.

CHAP. VIII.

A DRAWN BATTLE, WHICH ENDS IN WHAT IS VERY EXTRAORDINARY IN OUR DAYS----A COMPLETE VICTORY. A MATE OF AN INDIAMAN, NOT SO EXTRAORDINARY---A RASCAL.

THE Maratta forces had made an attack, with very superior numbers, on one of the quarters of our camp. My master, by the

the wifdom of his manœuvres, and his readinefs in executing them, foon erected the banners of victory over all the field.

It is impoffible to convey an adequate idea of a fcene like this by words. On our fide, rage, joy, avarice, and fwift-footed revenge, added cruelty to death, and fcattered every ftep with mangled carcafes. From the oppofite party, tumult, confufion, and terror, took away the very power of flight, or every other means of felf-prefervation. The helplefs foldier expofed his naked head to the horfeman's rage, and neither could preferve his life by feeble refiftance, or anxious intreaty.

I ATTENDED Hyder during the action and the flight, and I saw him perform at all times the office of an excellent general, and sometimes even the duty of an intrepid common soldier. It was hard to determine, whether the vigour of his body, or of his mind, was most to be admired. To shorten the view of such a disagreeable picture, I shall only add, that the Maratta general was taken, and his army almost all destroyed. My master, after a long pursuit, brought back his victorious troops in triumph, and sometime after, I attended him again to the apartment of the amiable Miss Melvil, who thus resumed her story.

I think, said she, illustrious Hyder, I have informed you of my intention of going to India, when the din of battle almost deprived me of my senses. I told my resolution to my aunt, who made a feeble effort to convince me that she was averse to it, though I very well knew, that nothing could, in reality, give her greater satisfaction. The preparations for my voyage were made, and you may now conceive me shut up in a small cabin, with only one maid servant, surrounded with stagnating air, and noisy sailors; an ocean extended beyond the reach of my eye, my only prospect; and all this, with a body distressed by sea sickness, and deprived of those conveniencies,
which

which female delicacy often stands in need of. The end which I promised myself by these sufferings, could alone give me courage to support them. An affair, however, occurred, that made the voyage even less pleasant than it would have been; I am sorry to take up your time by relating trifling incidents, but as they were once important to me, you have flattered me that that they will not be disagreeable for you to hear.

The first mate of our ship had often teased me with what he thought civility; and, while I considered his intentions merely as such, I believed myself under obligations to him. With the little

tle experience I then had, I could easily perceive a villanous heart under the smoothest surface. But as this was, at that time, an affair of much consequence to me, allow me, great Hyder, to give you the character of my new admirer.

We generally draw the sailor, boisterous in his behaviour, but honest and generous in his intentions. This was quite the reverse of this officer. His original education consisted in being able to read, write, and cast accounts. With a little navigation, added to these accomplishments, he considered himself as having reached the summit of science; and so qualified, he began the seafaring life.

life. He had already made two voyages to India, and as trade had succeeded under his management, he came to be of some consequence among his compeers. This was chiefly the effect of his extreme cunning, which never met with opposition to the success of its schemes, by any delicacy of conscience, or tenderness of heart. It was entertaining to hear the knave dwell on the last syllable of his words, while he thought the periods fell from his tongue like the soft whispering of a mid-day zephyr. His hair fell in ringlets on his shoulders, and he wore a black coat, with every other part of dress suitable to its decent gravity. The world attributed this negligence to the superiority of his mind;

mind; but I could easily trace it to its true source, where it sprung from one of the meanest desires of admiration, and the lowest wish to deceive. His face, by no means handsome, was contracted into a a heavenly meekness, mixed with self complacency, and his modest eye never ventured to look upon any person with confidence; but, to mark the humility of its master, was constantly fixed on its parent earth.

Thus adorned in mind and body, this mercantile sailor directed all the battery of his charms against me. He made love in the softest note of his scale, which I returned with distant civility only, as I knew I was in some measure
in

in his power. I observed one day he was particularly troublesome to me, as I walked the deck with my maid, for the benefit of the air. I little suspected the scene that was to ensue, and in which I was to be a principal actress.

My sailor, confident of success, and never suspecting that any woman could resist so many accomplishments as he had displayed, put into practice that very night, the stratagem, to which his behaviour had hitherto been subservient.

I had retired to bed very early, and was pleasing myself with the anticipation of expected happiness, when about twelve at night I heard

heard something unlock the door of my cabin. In a little afterwards, I saw a man enter, and come towards me, by the light that then remained. I had still resolution to keep quiet, when my lover coming up to my bedside, made many excuses for waiting on me at such an hour. From excuses he proceeded to actions, that raised my indignation and fear to such a pitch, that I cried out with all my force. The noise I made, awaked my maid in a fright, who without thinking any thing of the matter, roared out fire, fire! to the full extent of her lungs. She continued bellowing, until our cabin was quite full of passengers, officers of the ship, and sailors; nor did she stop, till her
mouth

mouth was shut by violence, that I might be able to give some account of the disturbance. With tears I told the whole truth to the company, who were now visible by the light of a candle which had been brought in. There stood the author of my misfortune, half undressed, for the torrent that entered, had allowed of no egress; and here, was a fat old lady in her shift, whom a sailor had drenched with a bucket of water; in the scuffle of entering, which he had brought for the purpose of extinguishing the supposed fire; some laughed, some scolded, and some were pleasant upon the occasion.

After this time, I never left my cabin till our arrival at Madras.

The Captain, who was always diftinguifhed for his humanity, and
what is more uncommon amongft
thofe men, for his learning, be-
haved with the utmoft tendernefs
to me during the remaining part
of the paffage; fending me provi-
fions, and every thing I could
ftand in need of, from his own table, and at his own expence.

THE hero of the affair, however,
did not repine under his difgrace;
but, taking advantage of his difap-
pointment, like a true genius, turned it to his own glory. As chafti-
ty was not one of the virtues that
intereft bade him affect, he fpoke
about his affair with me in a myf-
terious manner; plainly infinuating,
that he had come by my particular
appoint-

appointment, but that as I had neglected to acquaint the maid with the intrigue, upon her roaring out, it was necessary the mistress should join in the outcry, to prevent suspicion. This story was believed by all the female passengers, and gave me much unhappiness.

At length, however, we arrived at Madras, where I was received with the utmost pleasure by Capt. H—, my brother, and some other relations.

CHAP. IX.

TRUE GREATNESS OF MIND.---I GO TO CHINA, WHERE I SEE AN INSTANCE OF JUSTICE ON TWO ASTRONOMERS.---A CONSULTATION OF MEDICAL GENTLEMEN IN JAVA.

MY marriage, continued Miss Melvil, was only deferred for some time, on account of an expedition, which was undertaken againſt you, where both the captain

tain and my brother were obliged to attend.—It was judged proper to carry me along with them, as far as the town of Arcot, where I fell into your hands by the fate of war, and where every thing that was dear to me, was in one moment loſt for ever;—and on the very night, when marriage would have united my H. and me with ties that could never be looſened:—But death has for ever ſeparated him and my brother from the wiſhes of a helpleſs maid.

HERE Miſs Melvil diſſolved into tears. My maſter conſoled her with every tender promiſe he could make—It was long before ſhe could recover her-

herself so far as to answer a word.—At length she said, "You have already, illustrious Hyder, given sufficient proofs of the greatness of your mind; you cannot insult the unfortunate.— In return for foul treatment and black dishonour, I have received at your hands the gentlest usage, and the most fatherly affection.—The world may admire your virtues, but they cannot imitate them".

Hyder, at this moment hastily got up, and calling one of his officers, " go says he to Arcot, you will there find in the prison that faces the eastern gate, two English gentlemen,—let their chains be struck off, let them be pro-
" vided

" vided with every thing you may
" think agreeable as well as necef-
" fary, and let them have this
" money from me, with orders
" to come immediately to my
" camp."

I HAPPENED to be amongſt others
of my fellows, whom Hyder
ordered to be given to the Engliſh-
men.—I ſet out therefore with his
officer whom he had employed,
and in a few days we arrived at
Arcot.—When Hyder's pleaſure
was known, his meſſenger was
ſhown into the dungeon where the
two priſoners lay.

THEY had placed themſelves on
the ground, not far from a ſmall
crevice, where the entrance of a few
rays

rays of light served to give an idea of the horror of the place. Disappointment had so wearied out hope, that they took little notice of Hyder's officer on his entering, in, never imagining that it could be any other than the wretch appointed to sustain a miserable existence, by the necessaries which nature cannot want. They were talking of the sun-shine of former days, and comparing it with the clouds that at present, absorbed every ray of hope. I could see despondency strongly painted in both their faces, which bore the marks of the rapid progress of adversity, for they had nothing of that appearance, which misfortunes long continued will produce.

Hyder's

Hyder's officer at length broke filence, and informed them of the commands of his mafter, which they received with little apparent emotion. This was owing to the opinion they entertained of that prince, reckoning him a fubtle politician, to whom every method of advancing his own intereft was alike.—At this time I paffed into the poffeffion of one of the Englifh gentlemen, whofe heart I found lefs agitated concerning perfonal misfortunes, than for the lofs of a fifter, the fuppofed infolence of a conqueror, and the ignominy of defeat.

In fhort, my mafter and his companion were brought into the prefence of Hyder Alli.

EXPECTATION hovered over every heart, when Hyder looking at the young men, said, "I give you "both, from this moment, your "liberty, and what is infinitely "more, to the one I restore a "sister, to the other a wife who, "though possessed of beauty and "virtue above all her sex, a con- "queror, in spite of his right, "returns in her native innocence. "Take her young men, and learn "to know, that a native of the East "can be generous as well as brave. "—What can I say more."

At this moment Miss Melvil appeared.—But the mode that mortals have adopted of expressing ideas by words now fails me entirely; for

"Who

"Who can paint the lovers as they stood."

Let me draw a veil over such a tender scene, where such a variety of passions were visible in no common degree.— Hyder dismissed my master with his friend and sister, full of gratitude and admiration. I still attended these happy people, and I had the pleasure of remaining in their service till hymen had united the young pair, while pleasure sat smiling on the work.

From my present master, I passed into the hands of an Italian Jew, who gave me to an Indian manufacturer, by whom I was delivered to the captain of a trading vessel, and from him I passed into

into the hands of an English common sailor.

My new master about this time engaged with a vessel of the India company to go to China, where we arrived just in time to see Ha and Hum, two philosophers of great repute, hanged for neglecting to foretel an eclipse of the sun.— They were paid for this purpose by the state, to prevent the people from falling into superstition. I wonder, I said to myself, if philosophy be as well rewarded in in England.—I heard that philosophers starve in that country; it is surely better to hang them.

This was all I found remarkable in China, for I was
now

now in such bad company, I had little opportunity to make observations.

On our return, we touched at Batavia, where my master was seized with a remittent fever, for Van Frogan, to whom this island belongs, has been very careful to make it resemble his native element, which is neither air nor water. This he has done in direct opposition to the experience of many ages, as it was known before the days of Homer, that putridity is created by moisture, and made active by heat. The Grecians found it to their experience, and Van Frogan finds it to his experience, but he is far too wise to correct it.

A con-

A consultation of doctors from all the English ships was called on my master's case, for our surgeon began to find his conscience affected at the mortality that prevailed under his management. This I did not much wonder at, considering the numbers that died every day; but, I find now, that it was my want of experience which occasioned my wondering; for a doctor with a conscience about a matter of life and death, is a wonder; and to call in assistance without necessity, and of his own accord, is wonderful. But in truth reader, our surgeon, *from tenderness of conscience*, called a consultation of the faculty, and this is in reality a fact, whatever any person may pretend to assert to the contrary.

Mr.

Mr. Hypothesis first addressed the meeting, and after a long declamation against empyrics, he spoke as follows : " Fever, is evidently,
" gentlemen, produced by a spasm
" of the extreme vessels, which
" like sausages, are closed at the
" end, by the application of cold,
" or some other of the remote
" causes ; by these means the ex-
" pulsion of the contents is pre-
" vented. It is therefore my opi-
" nion, that the patient in ques-
" tion, should be made perspira-
" ble by sudorifics of the alkaline
" class." " You mistake the
" matter entirely," replied Mr. Outofuse, " fever, I assure you,
" depends on morbific matter,
" which manifests itself in the pu-
" trid discharges, &c. &c. There
" are

" are some cases where it will be
" said, that no morbific matter
" can have been applied to the
" body, as when fever has been
" produced by cold, debauchery,
" or the like; but gentlemen, as
" these instances militate against
" my theory, I shall take no no-
" tice of them, and therefore they
" signify nothing."

" Who can doubt," rejoined
Dr. Proportion," " of the propri-
" ety of venæsection; the moving
" powers will increase in the di-
" rect ratio of the diminution of
" the body moved, and what gen-
" tlemen are the moving powers,
" but the vis vitæ,; that is, life
" will be encreased by the ab-
" straction of blood, which is

" the

"the resistance to be overcome.
"Who has not heard, gentle-
"men, of a famous physician,
"who astonished a by-stander
"so much, with the happy effi-
"cacy of phlebotomy, that he
"cried out in extacy, " jugu-
"lasti febrem." Some will say,
"that this fever was not the
"same with the one before us,
"but to such men I answer no-
"thing. I candidly acknow-
"ledge, that of the vast number
"I have blooded in this climate
"for that fever, not one has re-
"covered; but I could observe
"such great alteration in the lead-
"ing symptoms, as might in-
"duce any reasonable man to
"repeat the experiment, and I
"am resolved to continue its
"use

"use. On the same principle
"of increasing the vis vitæ, I
"would apply blisters; for I
"have seen many patients de-
"prived of nearly all their skin,
"with the best effect, just be-
"fore their death. To prove
"gentlemen, the happy conse-
"quences of stimulating the vis
"vitæ, I myself, by the assistance
"only of a whip and a hair pin,
"encreased it so much in a gra-
"vid cat, that labour was brought
"on, and by a lucky delivery,
"I was enabled to save all the
"kittens. Here ended the consultation, without any thing being
determined.

THE surgeon's mate, by a proper use of the bark, recovered my
master,

master, although he could not account for the operation of his medicines. This he ventured to do without the knowledge or advice of his superiors, who were ever afterwards more confirmed in their first opinions, from the dispute I have related to you, my gentle reader.

CHAP.

CHAP. X.

I ARRIVE IN ENGLAND. MY MASTER SETS OUT ON A VISIT TO HIS MOTHER. A CONVERSATION WITHOUT ANY THING OF THE BON TON IN IT.

ABOUT the time that my master was perfectly recovered, our ship set sail for England. On our way, we touched at St. Helena, where the indolent inhabi-

inhabitants have been at little pains, to make the beſt of the few good ſpots that nature affords them. Our fleet almoſt exhauſted the whole proviſions on the iſland, and we left all the people, even the young ladies living on yams.

. On our arrival at Portſmouth, the bulk of the female innkeepers was the firſt phenomenon that ſtruck my attention; for ſuch moving heaps of humanity are not to be found elſewhere. My maſter was received by theſe people with the moſt flattering marks of diſtinction. With their aſſiſtance, and that of the ladies of eaſy virtue, who ſwarm in this town, he ſoon told out the laſt penny he
had

had earned in unhofpitable climates, after fix years of fatigue. In this reduced fituation, he no longer found refpect, where he before moved in a capital line. Adverfity opens the mind to virtue;—— Jack now recollected that he had an old mother, who lived in the north of England, whom he had not feen for many years. It wrung his heart to think, that he had nothing to give to fupport her feeble age. He refolved, however, to go and vifit her, and tell her his adventures.

As I was no longer a current coin, but a kind of curiofity, Jack refolved to keep me, for a prefent of true love, as he called it, to
Molly

Molly Black. This Molly Black had been Jack's companion in the earlier part of life, when mutual affection made them partners in all the labours of the field, as well as in the sports of the holiday. Like Lubin and Annette, they loved one another; and like them too, Jack, and Molly Black, demonstrated their love to each other in every possible way. But, to do my master justice, the desire of seeing his old mother, was the chief reason for his undertaking such a long journey. As soon as poverty allowed him to think, natural affection, like a torrent, bore down every argument that opposed its course.

WITHOUT

WITHOUT a sixpence in his pocket, you may now conceive Jack beginning his travels on foot, his heart very much at ease, since with his money, he not only lost his importance, but a load of business that attended it.

HE soon overtook, on the road, another traveller, who like himself, beat it away on the hoof, with a great blubberly, red-faced boy in his arms. Along with him, in a red cardinal, was the partner of his toils, through this vale of existence. She carried a bundle in her hand, with which, and the midday sun, for it was now July, she seemed to be much fatigued. My master, addressing the person with the child, "meffmate," faid he, "we can make but little way in this here weather; but if you will hand me your ballaft there, you may ride fomewhat the lighter." "I am exceedingly obliged to you for your charity, it is one of the cardinal virtues," anfwered the figure in black, at the fame time ftretching out the child to my mafter, who was going to take it into his arms, when it fet up fuch a bawling, as made both defift from the attempt. "But," continued the ftranger, "as Jacob will not leave me, if you'll take that burden from my wife for a little, you will beftow on me an equal favour; for the delicacy of the female form, is but ill

"qua-

" qualified for labour,"——(my
master immediately complied)—
" I was just thinking, when you
" came up to us, of what absolute
" importance the agency of that
" heat, which at present torments
" us, is in nature. Without it,
" air, water, and other fluids,
" would soon fix, and become so-
" lid. It is the plastic quality of
" that element, which covers the
" pool with insects, and the forest
" with leaves. Without heat the
" principles of form would exist
" in vain in the semen of animals,
" or the vegetable seed. As Lu-
" cretius, the Epicurean, on an-
" other occasion, sings

" Hinc

" Hinc alitur porro noſtrum genus atque
" forarum,
" Hinc lætas urbes pueris florere videmus
" Frondiferaſque novis avibus canere un-
" dique ſylvas."

Such an addreſs made me examine the perſon from whom it
proceeded, with greater attention.

He was a tall thin man. His
white, lank hair, fell in much dif-
order about his ſhoulders, which
were not bent by age, but by nature,
or long cuſtom. He wore a coat
and waiſtcoat of black cloth, which
were much ſoiled with ſnuff and
time. His breeches were of the
ſame colour, though of leather;
the hand of age had given them
nearly

nearly the properties of a looking-glafs, for their fhining furface, reflected the furrounding objects with confiderable perfection. His ftockings had been often, and badly darned, and contributed their evidence to give an idea of the poverty of their mafter. Jack, though he did not comprehend a word of the fpeech he had heard, anfwered to what the traveller had faid, " it is true, meff-
" mate;" and furveying him from head to foot with attention, " I
" fear, friend," continued he, " by
" your trim, your voyage has not
" been a fuccefsful one." " Very
" fuccefsful, and very pleafant;" replied the man in black, " though
" it is a little fatiguing, to travel
" as we do, on foot; efpecially
            " while

"while the rays of the sun are di-
"rect; but in return, we enjoy
"the full sight of every natural
"object that the country affords,
"and exercise, *sub jove*, is by far
"the most refreshing to both the
"mind and body. You must
"know, Sir, that this lady, who
"is my wife, and I, have been on
"a visit at Portsmouth, to her sis-
"ter, whom we have not before
"seen since our marriage. I have
"the honour to be a curate in
"Wales, but as my office does
"not bring me in above 10*l.* a
"year, out of which I have as
"many children to maintain, we
"judged it proper to come from
"that country on foot. This fine
"boy in my arms, is my son Ja-
"cob; as he was too young to be
"left

"left at home, I have carried him
"all the way from Wales; for,
"though I have had frequent of-
"fers, from well-difpofed perfons
"like yourfelf, to be eafed a lit-
"tle of the burden, the brat
"would never part from me, but
"always fets up fuch a bawling,
"as you have heard, whenever I
"attempted it." "That you may
"thank yourfelf for," interrupted
his wife, "for there was no necef-
"fity of bringing Jacob from
"home, he might have ftayed
"with Farmer Lewis's grand-mo-
"ther, who offered to keep him
"until our return." But you
"know, my dear," faid the hufband, "I have fo much pleafure in
"Jacob's company, that it has
"more than requited all my trou-
"ble.

"ble. The boy looks so sagaci-
"ously at the strange objects
"which surround him, that I
"dare say, his ideas are increas-
"ing every hour; and, what is the
"foundation of all our knowledge,
"but the impressions which are
"conveyed to the mind by the
"senses; which impressions will
"be in proportion to the oppor-
"tunities of acquiring them; so
"that in this light, neither Jacob's
"time, nor my labour, have been
"ill employed. But, my dear, it
"might have been prudent, as I
"observed on setting out, to have
"eased yourself of that bundle of
"finery, which has not only been
"a sore grievance to you, but even
"to me, as I could not assist you
"in carrying it, for Jacob"—At
this

this moment we arrived at the door of a small public house where our company agreed to take some refreshment.

CHAP.

CHAP. XI.

THE TRAVELLERS AGAIN ENTER INTO CONVERSATION ON THE ROAD---THEY ARE OBLIGED TO PART---AN INSTANCE OF GENEROSITY.

THE fare of my master and fellow travellers confifted of fome bread and ale. The parfon, as he had no money, ordered the landlord to bring him nothing but bread,

bread, obferving " that the ftaff of " life is bread;" but the good-natured publican made an addition of fome ale, anfwering from the fame facred writings, that " man " does not live by bread alone." In this manner, he informed us, he had been generoufly treated all the road; for, like a truly primitive Chriftian, he rather gloried in the want, than in the poffeffion of money.

After the refrefhment of fuch a banquet, the travellers again entered on the road, and no fooner had they bidden their landlord farewel, than the lady refumed the difcourfe. " My dear," faid fhe, " when we came to the inn, you " was blaming me for being at
" the

"the trouble of carrying these cloaths, not considering, I suppose, how necessary it is to make a proper appearance on a visit; for though you never chuse to change your coat, that will never excuse other people for not appearing genteelly.—But you have such a strange method of doing things, my dear, that your own interest seems the last object in view;—it is well known who wrote every sermon the bishop has preached for these twelve years, and for all that, your reward is as well known."

"Peace, woman," interrupted the parson, "the bishop has always been my good friend, and generous benefactor. Did not I recceive my present living from him?

"him? and, would he not have given me a better, had it not been for the refentment I expreffed againft young Squire Davies's whipper-in, for riding down my boy David. The young fquire, you know, oppofed me fo much, that the bifhop could not with propriety fulfil his kind intentions." Then addreffing my mafter.

"I think, friend," faid he, "I was telling you, that we have been at Portfmouth, where we met with a kind reception. My wife was for ftaying fome days longer; but, as I always tell her *eft modus in rebus*, fo we came away. Indeed, every body were fo fond of us, that I could

"could have tarried some time "longer with pleasure, but for my "impatience to get back to my "people, whom I never left so "long before. We have only a- "nother visit to pay in this neigh- "bourhood, to a gentleman, to "whose son I was tutor for six "years; as he never gave me any "thing for my trouble, but my "board, I am sure he will make "us very welcome; especially, "as I have not seen him for a "long time." My master, all this while, was silent, only answering now and then, " it is true." As for the parson, he never reflected but that his latin and hard words, were as familiar to Jack, as they had long been to himself. He always intermixed his discourse with sen-

tences

tences from the dead languages, without defign, or a wifh to raife himfelf in any body's opinion. Simplicity, with refpect to mankind, was the moft remarkable part of his character; which, in other refpects, really deferved admiration. He had an extenfive acquaintance with language, mathematics, and natural philofophy. On moft fubjects, his fentiments were fuch as every man fhould poffefs; for no one knew virtue, in theory, or practice, better than himfelf. To all his children, that were fufficiently old, he had given his turn of thinking, and as much as poffible of his knowledge; for he told us, " that however much people might blame him, in his circumftances to bring up a family

"ly in that ftyle, the knowledge
"of truth, he thought, could ne-
"ver be hurtful; and from the fa-
"cred writings he believed, that
"the feed of the righteous can ne-
"ver want bread."*

BEFORE night came on, my mafter wifhed thefe people a profpe-
rous voyage, for they were obliged
to ftrike off by a bye-road, to vifit
the gentleman I have already mentioned. All parties parted with

---

*. This account of the ftate of his mind, I received from my fubtle fpirit, DUCTILITY; who can look in-to nature as far as the celebrated Dr. Graham, author of fome excellent Theories on Generation.

G

marks of affection, the parson giving many thanks to my master, for the care he had taken of the bundle, which was now delivered to its proper owner. I soon lost sight of our companions, the wife sufficiently occupied with her fine things, and the husband with Jacob, whose bulk and contentment sufficiently shewed the extent of his health.

As, in the course of my travels, I afterwards learned something more of this blameless man, I believe it will not be disagreeable to my reader to hear it.

AFTER his return to Wales, his wife was constantly informing him of the insufficiency of his living, for

such

such a family, he, at length, resolved to make an effort to procure a better; which resolution, a favourable opportunity soon enabled him to put in practice. A living, in the gift of a Dr. S——, being accidentally vacant, the parson thought it an excellent time for him to apply. But he had no acquaintance with that gentleman, nor any interest that could give him a chance of success. He had often heard of the doctor's amiable character, and from this alone, he drew the presage of future fortune.

WITH such expectations, he set out for Dr. S——'s house, without informing his wife; who, most likely, knew too much of the world

world, to have given her confent to fuch an expedition. After a walk of twenty Welch miles, he got to the end of his journey, in his ufual fhabby coat; which, at this time, had the additional evil of being befpattered with dirt. A little before our parfon's arrival, Dr. S— had received a letter from the Earl of B—, recommending in the ftrongeft terms a gentleman of his own acquaintance to the living. Our adventurer knew nothing of this circumftance, which might have fhaken his hopes. He went boldly into the doctor's houfe, and fent up a letter he had wrote to him, conceived in very refpectful terms. In it, he informed him, that he was a curate with only ten pounds a year, with as many children

dren to maintain out of it. On this account, he humbly hoped, the doctor might confer on him the living, though he had brought no recommendation. He added, that as he was an honest man, he believed his presumption would be excused, which was the effect not of inclination, but of necessity. This extraordinary application made the doctor send for the author of it up stairs, with an invitation to stay dinner at his house. Though his appearance was so much against him, our parson displayed such a fund of knowledge, simplicity, and goodness of heart, that the doctor not only gave him the living in question, upon proper testimonies being produced of his good character, but also supplied him with money for defraying the expences of the institution.

CHAP.

CHAP. XII.

CHARACTERS ON THE TOP OF A STAGE COACH.——MY MASTER ARRIVES IN LONDON.——A PAWN-BROKER'S SHOP.

MY master, though he said little, felt a good deal at the departure of his fellow travallers; for the benevolence and sincerity of the parson were too remarkable to escape even his observation. How weak his powers in that way were, need not be told to thofe much acquainted with men of his clafs. He had been in India and China, and other parts of the eaft; he had vifited Holland, Portugal, and Turkey, without either obferving a difference in the countries, or the inhabitants; farther, than that he faw the men in India were black, that the Dutch had canals, and the Chinefe red and white houfes.

THE human brain is naturally in a ftate of apathy to thofe impreffions, for which education give it the higheft relifh. My mafter was quite the work of nature, a few prejudices excepted, which habit had

had strengthened beyond any possibility of altering.

Sometimes thinking of his mother, sometimes of the sea, and often comparing himself to the landsmen who passed us on the road, he jogged on the whole remainder of the day, in making but a very inconsiderable progress.

At length he put up, towards evening, in a small ale-house, where mutual feelings induced him and the landlord's daughter to sleep out the night in the same bed. By her interest, in the morning, he got a place on the top of a stage coach, for London, which stopped regularly at that house for a little freshment to the driver. It happened, very luckily for my master, that this Phaeton, who never drove his steeds till his precordia were surrounded with liquid fire, was rather behind hand in the payment of his morning dose, which had the good effect of making him civil to passengers, especially such as were recommended at a watering place.

I shall give a short picture of the personages that now surrounded my master, in the belief, that my reader thinks with me, that human nature, in every state, is worthy the attention of a man.

The

The most remarkable figure on the top of the coach was, an Irish tar; who distinguished himself greatly by the length, the loudness, and the volubility of his orations. He had received several wounds in the service, and though a young man, was in expectation of getting into one of the hospitals on that account.

At his back sat a woman of a singular character. She still wore a sufficient appearance of youth, to demonstrate that she was not old. —But she was meagre and wasted. —A wicked life was strongly imprinted in her countenance, which by degrees had assumed the character of the mind. I could discover, that she was one of those unfortu-

nate females, who fall a prey to the passions of men, before they know the value of that virtue which they never can recal. She had been present at several engagements in the West Indies and America, where she had fought on board a ship of war, performing every office of a seaman with skill and courage. So well had she acquitted herself, that she received the proportion of a man, on a division of prize money. She was now on her return to London, in possession of nothing but her glory, for she was as poor as when she had left it. Behind this Amazon, sat an old meek Jew, whose beard had extended considerably beyond its usual dimensions as this was one of the occasions of self-denial.
This

This man seemed very much a knave in spite of the honey of his speech. I think I never saw a more striking contrast than the two last characters afforded; which the lady did not fail to heighten, by language addressed to the Israelite, that decency forbids us to relate. She professed herself highly captivated with his wig, his religion and his beard, and she gave him many an invitation to try his abilities, while herself should stand the judge. He was afraid to answer one word, and only durst signify his disapprobation, by moving as far as possible from his antagonist.

The Irishman did not fail to improve so favourable an occasion, for the disaster of his limbs had

not

not destroyed his inclination for sport.. As Abraham was placed with his back to the lady, he, very carefully introducing his hand between them, gave her a severe pinch in the midst of one of her soliloquies on the very great utility of that law of Moses, which sayeth, "neither shalt thou marr "the corners of thy beard". This she never doubted was bestowed on her by the Jew, when turning round, with eyes like two pieces of lighted charcoal, she seized the trembling Israelite, and imprinted on his face not a few tokens of her resentment, while the unhappy culprit remained ignorant of the cause of such a sudden storm. —But it is needless to give more instances of this sort of en-

tertain-

tertainment, which afforded my master the warmest satisfaction; for besides the fun, as he called it, one of his earliest and strongest prejudices was his hatred of a Jew.

Upon our arrival at London, my master fell in with some of his East-India messmates.—He could not deny himself a little grog with those honest fellows. But his finances were so absolutely reduced, that in order to accomplish this, he carried two shirts, which he had in a bundle, and at length myself, to a pawn brokers shop in Holborn. The shirts he left with much pleasure, but I could see his pain on producing me; for the idea of Molly Black,

to

to whom he now had nothing left to give, returned in its full vigour.

The melancholy air of my new habitation, and the dark countenance of my prefent poffeffor, combined to infpire me with a fort of horror I had never known before.

Gentle reader, if it is not very difagreeable to you, the view of fuch a place may be attended with inftruction. It will teach you to know what wretches feel.—You will learn to efteem the fun fhine of your own condition, and difcontent, fo injurious to the deity, will feldom hang over your forehead."

First then, take a view of that window, where such a variety of trinkets are displayed.—Those watches that were wont to mark the course of chearful hours, are now silent as the lapse of time, which they were designed to measure. They point at different parts of their circle you see, according as they were last animated by their unfortunate masters.—That ring was perhaps in remembrance of the purest flame that love can excite, and may have been worn by some gentle maid.—This one is a wedding ring; it has been a witness of the fairest pleasures that heaven bestows on mortals.—Sad misfortunes alone could force its mistress to expose it to sale; perhaps this step was the only to one by which she
could

could support the helpless offspring of that union it was made to celebrate.

On the other side of the apartment, you behold the very necessaries of life, which hunger has torn from their masters. Good heavens! what has become of those wretches which these rags used to defend from the inclemency of the weather. This is not a temple where wealth has deposited its superfluities; it is a cell loaded with the spoils of the afflicted, and the very necessaries of necessity.

CHAP.

CHAP. XIII.

HISTORY OF THE PEOPLE I SAW IN THE PAWNBROKER'S SHOP.

WHEN I entered this abode, it was illuminated with a great number of lamps, for the sun by this time had left the world in darkness, and the beasts of the field, more wise than men, were enjoying the refreshment of sleep, and the luxury of dreams.

The first customer that entered our shop, was a young woman with much of the lady in her appearance. Round her eyes a degree of purple tinge, joined with the watery look of the eye ball, which moved heavily in its orbit, seemed to indicate with other things, that she was not unacquainted with sorrow.—She seemed on entering, to feel much for the situation into which necessity had thrown her, but rousing all her fortitude, she advanced to our counter, and producing a gold watch, received from my master a small sum in proportion to its real value.

I HAD a desire to know more of this young person's history, for I strongly sympathised in her sufferings,

ferings which did not seem to me the consequence of any fault. For this purpose I dispatched Ductility, one of my subordinate spirits, to follow her home and learn her history.—I had the following account, on the return of my messenger.

THIS lady, is the daughter of a merchant, who was eminent in London for his great wealth. She married *against the will* of her father a young man of much merit, and no fortune, which the parent ever afterwards esteemed such a crime, that all he had was given at his death to a nephew, whom the uncle never saw in his life time.—After her father's death, the unhappy daughter beheld

held her family increafe, without the hopes of being able to fupport them, when she loft her hufband, after a long illnefs, occafioned by the reflection on his fituation.—She hitherto had not applied to any of her ungenerous relations; but as this watch was almoft the only thing betwixt her children and want, fhe muft foon fuffer the pangs that await a generous mind, when forced to folicit what fhould have been offered unafked.—This is not the only inftance I have feen of the bad confequences of rafh marriages, nor the only one I have known of the hard hearts of old men.

THE lady was fcarcely gone, when an old warriour came in. He
had

had left his legs in Germany, and was now supported by two wooden substitutes. Under his coat was concealed a broad sword, which with much unconcern, he informed my master, he would be glad by his assistance to convert into porter. " This liquor, said he, gave vigour
" to my youth, and at present sup-
" ports my old age. You see,
" gentlemen, I have few limbs to
" take care of, and no children,
" and why should not I make the
" best use of my time. The peo-
" ple at Brussels, where I was quar-
" tered, are much wiser than you
" Englishmen, for they neither
" learn any thing, nor do any thing.
" —This sword, gentlemen, has
" killed a Frenchman before now,
" and shall yet enable me drink
" the

" the health of our King, and
" old England." The warriour,
on getting a little money, went a-
way exceedingly well contented,
as he was now in a fituation to
pleafe both himfelf, and his
friends.

Our next cuftomer was a W—,
that left with us a valuable cruci-
fix, which fhe ftole from a French
Abbè, the author of a treatife on
morality. It muft be acknow-
ledged, that the Abbè had given
her opportunities to accomplifh
the theft, which he fhould not
have given.

A young gentleman next made
his appearance. As his figure was
one of the fineft and moft ftriking I
had

had ever seen, I was inſtantly ſeized with a deſire of knowing his hiſtory. One of my ſubordinate ſpirits immediately mounted his cella turcica by my command, from which ſpot the brain above may be ſeen marked with impreſſions, like the figures on a celeſtial globe. Theſe impreſſions are nothing but the ſcratches made by objects which have been preſented to the ſenſes, and of which memory makes uſe in her operations. By reading theſe, we can diſcover all the tranſactions of any conſequence in which a man has been engaged. I ſay of any conſequence, for the leſs material impreſs with ſo little force, that the marks they leave, are in time entirely obliterated. But to proceed, I diſmiſſed Ductility, a very

very subtle spirit, who went away safely mounted on the cella turcica of that gentleman, who left us, after getting some money in exchange for a few trinkets. The most remarkable parts of his story are as follow.

Mr. W——, a gentleman of ancient family, and considerable fortune, sent his second son to Cambridge, with the view of bringing him up in the ecclesiastical line, and with the hopes of soon seeing him a bishop. Young W. on his entering the fields of philosophy, made such a rapid progress, that it was every where believed that no path of science was too rugged for his genius to overcome. After being there for several years, he
came,

came, by the consent of his father, to London, to pass away a few months of vacation from abstruse speculation. The scholar found himself, at first, at a loss to join as he wished, in the entertainments of the town. He did not know the forms of the beau monde, nor the etiquette of fashionable manners. But as a man may perceive the superiority of his figure and understanding above others, and yet possess no vanity, so young W. soon found out, that nature and education gave him a better title to shine than most of his companions.—A very few weeks after acquiring confidence in himself, made him master of all the fashionable mysteries, which he had believed, on the credit of his bon ton companions, were of the moſt difficult acquiſition. The converſation of his friends was without variety, a mere rotine of lively chit chat. Their wit, when that was attempted, had no purity, and even their politeneſs, was the ridiculous execution of a few forms, to which cuſtom had given a ſanction. W. did not neglect the modes in vogue of being agreeable, but as moſt of theſe are founded in reaſon, he applied them with reaſon; never looſing ſight of this important truth, that good breeding is the art of never giving offence. The ſcholar and the beau formed in him ſuch an agreeable compound, that W. now became the talk of the ladies of wit; who ſtamped a value on him for the ladies of no wit.

wit. His good nature that strongly shewed itself in a good face, gave him not a few admirers, which the genteel figure his father enabled him to make, contributed much to increase. Intoxicated with success, he neither thought of Cambridge nor Aristotle. He was well received through all the circle of beauty, without feeling even a temporary passion; for his vanity was so far elevated with success, that it almost destroyed every feeling of that nature.

WHILE his mind was in this situation, he saw one evening, at Ranelagh, the young Countess of ———, with her father, who were just arrived from Rome, and on their way to the North proposed staying

staying a few days in London.—
W. introduced himself amongst
the groupe that were congratulating
his lordship on his safe arrival in
England, and found means to
converse with the countess, who
soon compleated by her conversation, the conquest which her
beauty had begun. It now occupied all his attention to get better
acquainted with her, for his love
increased in proportion, as he
found difficulty in approaching
her. He saw a thousand obstacles
to surmount, which opposed his
unhappy passion. Though she was
young, good sense and a considerable share of experience effectually guarded her against any
foolish attachment. Besides this,
she

she was much his superior in point of fortune and rank.—

WHILE he was agitated with such reflections as these, the short time passed away that the countess had to remain in London.—He placed himself in the way that her coach took on leaving the town, and after making a respectful bow as she passed, retired to his lodgings, with as heavy a heart as ever was made so by love.

CHAP. XIV.

PAWN BROKER'S SHOP CONTINU-
ED.---A LORD, AND A SOLDIER
---NEITHER OF THEM UNCOM-
MON CHARACTERS.

WHAT will not love suggest to its votaries! W— had heard that the chief motive of the countess's father, for going abroad, was the recovery of his health, which, he always imagined, was

in a declining ftate. He was one of thofe hypochondriacs, who with better fenfe than other men, in this refpect difcover a degree of folly that aftonifhes fools. He was continually reflecting on the wonderful machinery that compofes a man. The inflammation of parts, the rupture or obftruction of veffels, was conftantly in his mind. He had already felt moft difeafes in imagination, which the body is fubject to in reality. An eafterly wind, or any accident, however infignificant, would put him out of all order. Such was the peculiarity of this nobleman; —in other refpects he poffeffed the beft judgment. His learning was extenfive, and his humour, when
he

he happened to forget his ailments, was infinite.

Young W— resolved to turn this biass of his lordship's mind to his own advantage. He had some knowledge of the theory of medicine, and hoped to introduce himself under the character of a physician: for he knew that every other species of men, was become disagreeable to that nobleman.

To put this design into execution, he provided himself with proper cloaths, and as decent a wig as ever hypocrisy appeared in. Thus equipped, he set out for his lordship's seat; where he announced himself a physician, whom the desire of improvement induced to travel,

travel, and at this time to visit his lordship, whose fame in that divine art he was well acquainted with. No compliment could be more welcome than this, and the doctor was received with much respect. They immediately began to converse on the healing art. His lordship had only time to go thro' some of the aphorisms of Sanctorius, when the entrance of his daughter interruped the discourse.

" Can you believe," said his lordship, addressing the countess,
" that this worthy physician is al-
" ready eighty years of age."
" Indeed my lord," she replied,
" I should not take him to be a-
" bove eighteen." " But I can
" assure you it is true, he knows
" the

" the secret of Paracelsus, by
" which human life can be pro-
" tracted to any period, and youth
" and beauty renewed;—such are
" the effects of that wonderful
" science of chymistry,—for, doc-
" tor, I would no longer have it
" called an art. When it was in
" the hands of men, who, by mere
" chance made mixtures and ap-
" plied heat; or, when mixtures
" were made, and heat applied by
" rule, as is the case to this day
" with the apothecaries in Lon-
" don,—chymistry was an art.
" But chymists of knowledge can
" now look a little way into effects
" and causes, and are able to refer a
" number of phenomena to a par-
" ticular principle. In this way
" the power of man over matter is
" en-

" encreased, which is the ultimate
" end of all useful philosophy."

WITH such discourses as these, his lordship and the doctor passed the whole afternoon, the latter, in spite of his silence, being scarcely able to conceal his ignorance.

AT last, the long wished for moment arrived, when his lordship left the room, and the young countess remained alone with the doctor, whom her eyes could never convince was the same Mr. W—, she had heard so much of in London, and for whom she had already conceived an attachment. He discovered immediately his real name, implored her forgiveness, and told her of the violent passion he felt for her. He asked
a thou-

a thousand pardons for the strange method he had taken to see her, and pleaded his cause so effectually, to a judge already prepossed in his favour, that he soon obtained a pardon for his offence.

AFTER remaining eight days with his lordship, to whom he discovered the secret of Paracelsus, he went away, with vows of eternal fidelity to the countess, whose pleasure in being with him, nothing but the idea of deceiving her father could abate. She promised to visit London in about a month; where W— returned again, with all the joy of success.

THE news of the splendour of young W—'s appearance, with his
extra-

extravagance, could not long be concealed from his father, who was not ignorant that such a course was very contrary to the interest of his son, who had little fortune to support it. He therefore wrote him several times to return to the university. Though he had received very respectful letters from his son, in answer to these, yet he was convinced, that the only way to make them have any effect, was to stop his remittances; this he had done, a month before our young gentleman had gone to the country on the expedition where we have already followed him. Ever since that time, his expences were obliged to be much contracted, for he resolved to live in town, till he could again see the lovely countess, tefs, who conſtantly occupied his thoughts.

As it is above a month ſince ſhe promiſed to be in London, he is obliged to put up with circumſtances, that no paſſion, but love, could make him ſupport. This very poverty, was the occaſion of his viſiting my maſter, for the dreams of pleaſure that the counteſs has excited, are not yet diſpelled by diſappointment.

My ſpirit adds, that juſt before he could diſengage himſelf from the membranes that ſurround the brain, Mr. W. received the following letter from his miſtreſs, every word of which gave his brain ſuch violent ſhocks, that the bones had much

merit

in hindering the expulsion of their contents.

SIR,

"THE death of my father has prevented me from being in town, according to my intention. If you love me, as you have said, come down immediately, for I confess no company can be more agreeable. I have now an estate to dispose of, and am free of all engagements with respect to myself.

Your's, &c.

THE

THE next gentleman that entered our shop, was an officer of the army, with three curls on each side of his head, which were highly powdered and scented. Though he was very young, his face was round and large, with a belly somewhat prominent, a certain sign of ease. He seemed very much pleased with himself.—I thought, and would have said with Shakespear,

"What pity 'tis you want a pouncet box."

but you know I cannot speak.— After smiling in our looking-glass, he bought a breast-pin set with diamonds. He put it into his shirt, looked at himself once more, and strutted out.

I IM-

I IMMEDIATELY difpatched my worthy fpirit Fufibility to read the marks in his brain that had given ideas. In half an hour my meffenger returned. I chid him for ftaying fo long, for the time he took was more than fufficient to examine the records of the longeft life. "And "what have you found, deferving "of fo much trouble?" faid I. "I "found nothing," anfwered the fpirit. "This man has no ideas, "and never had any." "But "have you examined thoroughly? "I have entered every cavity," replied Fufibility, "of his brain; "I have paffed through the mi- "nuteft pipes, and inveftigated "its moft fubtle convolutions;— "and all is as plain as a mirrour : "—no impreffions—no marks of "ideas,

"ideas, I assure you. Last of all,
"I crept into the pineal gland,
"which, you know, is the cham-
"ber of the soul, where I found
"it a-sleep, and it has never once
"awakened since he was born."

CHAP.

CHAP. XV.

HISTORY OF FLORA.

MY spirit had just finished this extraordinary account, when my attention was called to one of the loveliest girls I had ever seen. She was plain, clean, and neatly dressed, with such a degree of simplicity in her looks, that the

the account I received of her gave me a real pain.

FLORA is the daughter of a wealthy farmer in Yorkſhire, who gave her a good education in the country, as ſhe had been engaged by an old juſtice of the peace, who found, on calculation, that he ſhould need a nurſe by the time Flora was ready for marriage. But love which pervades the univerſe, attached Flora as ſtrongly to Simmons, a neighbour's ſon, as Simmons was attached to her.

THE firſt interruption to their blifs, for blifs they poſſeſſed in each other's company, was a place of clerk to a manufactory, which a friend of old Simmons had pro-
cured

cured for his son in London. The two young lovers parted with many a tear on either side, and the strongest promises of eternal fidelity.—Flora vowed that no intreaties of her father should make her marry the justice, and Simmons protested that no damsel in London should make him forget Flora.

Simmons was not long settled in London, before he found that his honest industry would enable him to maintain a wife in a frugal manner, and he wrote the glad tidings to Flora. It was agreed that she should come up to London, without acquainting any person of her intention, as she knew her father would never be prevailed upon to give his consent, and she put her

I scheme

scheme into execution, under pretence of visiting a relation who lived at some distance; she took a place in a stage coach and soon arrived in London with a joyful heart. Simmons was not at the inn where her stage arrived, as he had promised; a circumstance, from which she foreboded no good.— She sought out his lodgings, and found him in the last stage of a putrid fever.---He looked at her without being able to speak, and while he gazed, he expired in her arms.

Poor Flora was now in a situation truly deplorable; but she thought not of herself, the idea of him she had lost took entire possession of her mind. But she did
not

not long enjoy the power of feeling, for disease soon destroyed all sensation. After the rudest shocks of it were over, she returned by degrees to her senses, when she found herself in the same bed where she saw Simmons expire. An old woman sat beside her, and with every mark of benevolence, administered the necessaries of which she stood in need.

One day when Flora was a little better than usual, and just able to sit up supported by pillows, her nurse addressed her as follows.

"My pretty young lady, it
"gives me the sincerest pleasure to
"see you so far recovered.—We
"have all been under the most
"dread-

"dreadful apprehensions for your
"safety. It would, to be sure,
"break any heart to see such a
"lovely creature distressed in this
"manner. But my pretty young
"lady, what do you design to do
"when you have got well again,
"for if you return to your father
"before you make some conditions
"with him, he will certainly give
"you to that justice I have heard
"you speak about. I therefore
"think you should write him
"from London, and I will give
"the letter to a relation of mine,
"who will deliver it himself, and
"remonstrate with your father.
"But as the people of this house
"expect payment for their lodg-
"ings, you shall go to a friend's
"house of mine my pretty young
"lady,

" lady, where you shall live hap-
" pily, and without expence, till
" you have an answer from the
" country."---With such speeches
as these, this infamous old wretch
prevailed on the simple Flora, to
consent to her proposal of going to
the house of one of those women,
who support themselves by admi-
nistering to the lusts of mankind.
Before she left her present lodgings, she paid three times as much
for them, as in justice she should
have done, and the remainder of
her fortune she gave to her old
nurse, to keep for her until such
time as she should want it.

Her new landlady received her
in the kindest manner, making a
a long discourse, where the words

chris-

christianity, charity, and feeling, often occurred. Flora was now as happy as her late misfortune would allow, and penetrated with gratitude to the good people, she thought it her duty to appear chearful.

ONE afternoon, a gentleman, whose name was Traffic, paid a visit to Mrs. Black, with whom Flora now lived. This gentleman was thought a very proper person, on account of his great wealth, to purchase the charms of innocence; for he is one of the *best men* on 'change; which character he has been able to acquire by indefatigable attention to business, and by being void of those little feelings of generosity, which will at times lead others to do things

things contrary to their interest.—
The credit of his purse gives him
authority and apparent respect, and
on that credit he can often lord it
over needy merit, which is glad to
bear with him in hopes of his af-
sistance. But he never had a real
friend, and never will have one.
—He never was beloved, and will
die unregretted.— Such was the
person designed to compleat poor
Flora's ruin.—To one less experienced than Mrs. Black, this man,
who was both old and ugly, might
have appeared a very improper
object to beguile the heart from
virtue.—But Mrs. Black knew her
business, and did not dispair of success.

Mr. Traffic, after making a few

dry

dry obfervations, and taking fome liberties with Flora, which nothing but the fear of offending fo great a man in the houfe of her benefactrefs made her fuffer, concluded his firft vifit, with a promife to return as foon as bufinefs would allow. When he was gone, Flora's friend harrangued much on his great worth, and infinite riches. " I wifh my dear girl, faid
" fhe, that Mr. Traffic would take
" a liking to you. I am fure it
" would be the making of all your
" relations, for no body has more
" intereft than he. He is befides
" a proper man enough, and I
" know he has a fweet temper.
" Don't you think your father
" would rejoice at your good luck,
" ---all the affair of your going
" away

"away would then be lost in the joy of your success." — I am sorry madam, said Flora, "that I cannot see this gentleman with the same eyes that you do; indeed I think him very ugly, and from his look I should believe him to be very ill tempered. As to a husband, I can never think of one after my dear Simmons, for though he had not much money, nor perhaps what the people of London speak so much about, interest; he was a sweet creature, nor shall I ever find his like again.---Oh! madam, had you seen him when we parted;---when he hung on my arm." A flood of tears, which the innocent Flora poured forth on the recollection of her former happiness,

piness, put an end to the conversation for the present.

With such discourses as these, this infamous woman endeavoured to prepossess poor Flora with a good opinion of the merchant, who thus hoped to purchase his pleasure on the easiest terms. But this wicked pair found Flora's virtue as strong as her simplicity was great. No reasoning could make her entertain a good opinion of Mr. Traffic, whose native rusticity, and habitual haughtiness, were but ill calculated to please a a young woman of virtue.

When it was found that Flora was thus obstinate under gentle usage, it was resolved to have recourse to

that

that of a different nature. Mrs. Black came in one day, just as Flora had quarrelled with her admirer for taking liberties which she thought indecent, "it is a very "pretty return said she, for the kind "treatment you have received at "my house. My friends can no "longer visit me for your rude "behaviour. But I deserved as "much, for people should take "care whom they prevent from "starving or beggary." Flora was astonished at this address; "I am "very sorry madam, she replied, "for having given you any of- "fence, for I am sensible of the "favours you have bestowed upon "me, which you did without my "even asking them at your hands. "—But still, I cannot think that I

"was

"in danger of starving or beggary. —But since things have turned out in this way, continued she, weeping, I shall leave your house immediately, if you will assist me in getting back to my father?" "With all my heart, answered Mrs. Black, the sooner the better to be sure, but I expect to be paid for the trouble and expence you have put me to, by living in my house above a fortnight; you don't surely think that people in London give board and lodging for nothing." Flora willingly agreed to the payment, but upon enquiry, she could get no account of her nurse, to whom she had given her whole fortune. It was in vain to plead that her father would pay her expences,

pences, her landlady was inexorable, and insisted for money immediately, or that Flora should go to prison, to spend the remainder of her life amongst cheats and sharpers. While things were in this situation, Mr. Traffic by design entered the room. He upbraided Mrs. Black in the strongest terms for her barbarous behaviour. "Flora says "he, you shall go with me; I will "take care of you till you get back "to your father, and I shall pay "this lady the mighty sum about "which she makes such an outcry." Flora was once more deceived.— She assured him she forgave him all his offences, which such a good man could never have meant to give in reality; she called him her

gene-

generous benefactor, and telling him how happy her father and all her little sisters would be on her return, she went with him to the door, where they stept into a coach together.

But I shall leave the remainder of this black transaction in the darkness that at present surrounds it, and only tell the public, that Flora, in spite of all her virtue, fell into the snare of her seducer, from which she could never extricate herself. May this story remain as a caution to youth, that no purity of intention will justify imprudence. Flora is now discarded by the merchant, and when she entered our shop it was to sell the few

few things she could spare from immediate use to in order to take a a place in the stage coach; for with the truest penitence of heart, she is resolved to return to her father.

CHAP.

CHAP. XV.

THE YOUNG DIVINE.---THE NO-BLEMAN OF VENICE.

AFTER Flora had left our shop, a young man came in with a cane, which he exchanged with my master for a guinea.

HE is an Oxford divine, but having come to town chiefly *ad ex-purgandos*

purgandos renes, he has caught an infection that shall be namelefs. The guinea he received from my mafter, he defigns to lay out on Dr. Leake's pills, for he is heartily tired of his furgeon; who, to tell you the truth, gentle reader, has lengthened out his patient's cure, in the fame proportion with his own bill. The poor ftudent has already paid an account of ten pounds, which fum he received from a maiden aunt, to affift his ftudies, and buy books of divinity; for, next to a favourite cat, he is the object of her earthly affection. I am afraid he wont mend the matter by Dr. Leake's affiftance, for I fwear by the purity of my fubftance, that there is only one thing in nature that can be depended on

in

in this case, and that is, the more efficacious the more simple its preparation.—We dont want remedies, but take my word for it, reader, we want heads to apply them.

The croud of customers that succeeded this gentleman, do not deserve to be particularized. They were, in general, the wretched offspring of vice and dirt. Extreme necessity brought some, and others came to change their best cloaths for a little money, to purchase a dose of aqua vitæ, or Roman purl.

An aged man drew my attention more than the rest. His toothless jaws were grinding the
frag-

fragments of a ftale potatoe, which the cold hand of charity had beftowed upon him. " What do you want " friend?" exclaimed my mafter. " Here, Sir," replied the worn-out man, " here are two fhirts my " fon left behind him, when he " was impreffed into the fea fer-" vice. He is now gone, and can-" not fupport his father, who is " not able to provide for himfelf." This venerable piece of wretchednefs, was deprived of his fon, in confequence of a partiality that a Welch man of fortune entertained for his fon's wife.

THE next remarkable perfon that appeared, was evidently not a native of Great Britain. His face was much burned by the fun, and

and he had that peculiarity of speech, feature, and dress, which distinguishes the Italians. He had no sooner disposed of some fine miniature heads, and a few medals of gold, all of which he gave away with much reluctance, than he went out, but not before I had mounted a spirit as usual on his cella turcica. He had but just left our shop, said my messenger, when accident put into his way an old acquaintance. After surprize allowed him the power of motion, he rushed into the arms of the stranger,— "My dear Signor Tedeschi," says he, "Heaven has at length grant- "ed my wishes, for I see you a- "live, and in the land of liber- "ty." "Signor Antonio," replied

plied his friend, with eyes shining in tears, "this is more than could well be born, though I had been prepared for the interview. Words cannot convey to my dear Antonio the joy and feelings of my heart. But let us proceed to my house, which, from this moment, is equally yours, and there we shall have time to satisfy each other's curiosity." "First let me fly to inform my wife of the good news, for Signor Tedefchi, that amiable woman has left her country for ever to attend me." "I was afraid, my friend, to enquire about the Lady Francifca, in cafe death, or the accidents that attend an escape like yours, might have deprived you of the best

"of

"of wives. I congratulate you again on your happiness," continued Tedeschi, "let us not wait a moment longer, I am tortured with impatience to see her."—The two friends adjourned to an inn, where the Lady Francisca was made a partner in their happiness. After discharging the bill, they all took coach to the house of Signor Tedeschi. My spirit was so enchanted with such a scene of pleasure, that he could not leave it, but remained in his lurking place, till he should inform himself from their own mouths of their different histories.

AFTER the most hearty welcome on the part of Signor Tedeschi, he told his friend of his great desire fire to hear the ſtory of his eſcape. "For my part," ſaid he, "I have long imagined, that Signor Antonio had gone to the land, where the ungrateful Venetians ſend every man that feels the fire of liberty, or diſtinguiſhes himſelf, as you have done, by glorious actions." "It is not," anſwered Antonio, "the Venetians that I am obliged to for my preſervation, for they have done every thing in their power to deprive me of my life. But it will be proper, in order to give you a clear idea of the whole buſineſs, to begin my ſtory at that period when you left our tyrannical country.

I NEED

"I NEED not inform you, my friend, how popular I was in Venice, at the expiration of my government in Albania. My name was every where whispered among the people, who considered me as a protector of liberty, and a friend to trade. But the complete victory I obtained over a body of Turks, with the honourable peace I concluded for Venice, were crimes that our government could never forgive. I saw myself surrounded with spies at my house on the Brent, as well as in Venice, and I was denied all the privileges of my ancestors, 'till my conduct should be examined. Is was in this situation that I applied to you to carry my wealth to England, where I knew you had lodged that immense

K fortune

fortune your father acquired, as a banker. I was then in hopes of being able to escape in a few days for that country; for I did not suspect that my confinement was so strict, as I soon discovered it to be. You was scarcely under sail in the Dutch vessel, before your whole transaction with me was known, and above ten thousand spies were in search of you through Venice.

"On that very night, I was seized, with my wife, in the square of St. Mark, on our return from an assembly, where most of the Venetian nobility were present, and I was immediately thrown into a dark dungeon, up to the knees amongst putrid water. Thus in less than

than an hour, after being one of the greatest noblemen in Venice, I became the first wretch in the universe.

"I HAVE often wondered, Signor Tedeschi, that those noblemen who condemned me,——with most of whom I was educated, with many of whom I had always lived in the strictest friendship—I say, I have often wondered, how these men could pass the night with such happiness in my company, whom, they knew, in a few hours, was to be in such a horrid situation, by their own decree. I received as much civility at the ball from every person present as usual, and the Doge's lady favoured me with her hand in our dances.

"SUCH

"Such is the effect of politics on the human heart, at least such is the effect of politics in Italy. The imperfections in every constitution give such room to those that move the wheels of government and so many temptations of being wicked, that a good man in such a character, is not enough to be admired. The unequal execution of laws in every state——But, continues Signor Antonio, I fear much we may have been overheard. My warmth has carried me too far. I have said more than would hang any Venetian, after a life of the greatest virtue.

"There is no fear, answered his friend laughing, you are now in a land of liberty. You are in Britain,

tain, the only country in the world where men live in a state worthy of the dignity of their being. This happy land shall shine for ever in the historian's page, a glorious instance of the blessings that freedom bestows. Though I am an Italian, like yourself, my greatest boast shall ever be, that as a Briton, I can feel my heart beat at the very name of liberty."

CHAP. XVII.

THE HISTORY OF THE NOBLEMAN OF VENICE CONCLUDED.

"BLEST country, replied Signor Antonio, the refuge of mortals from oppreſſion.—Surely Britons cannot know the extent of their own happineſs, which experience enables me to ſee from compariſon in its ſtrongeſt colours!

"But to continue my story: I found myself, as I have said, in a dark dungeon, up to the knees in putrid water. This you know is the place where thofe unfortunate men are allowed to perifh, who have uttered any thing, whether in praife or difpraife, of the government of Venice. I had heard that thofe wretches, who could procure any fpirituous liquor with their food, would live in this fituation a fortnight, and fometimes for three weeks. Faint hopes that my deliverance might be fomehow effected induced me to try the experiment, and I protracted a miferable exiftence, in this way, for twelve days, enjoying a little fleep at intervals, by leaning againft the wall. At length,

length, I had given up all expectation of deliverance. The pains that affected my body, and the putrid stench, that came from the corpses of the numerous wretches that had perished in this dungeon, where they still lay, became quite intolerable. I had just resolved to drown myself, by lying down on the floor, when my jailor entered, about midnight. " Signor An-
" tonio," said he, " I pity
" your sufferings, and if you will
" follow me, we may perhaps
" escape. Dont look astonished,
" for though there never was an
" instance, before this time, of
" humanity in a goaler of Venice,
" I am resolved to hazard all on
" your account. Follow me, Sig-
" nor, your wife, to whom you
" owe

"owe your preservation, awaits you hard by, in a gondola." I was astonished at what I heard, and imagined it was a chimera of my exhausted brain, just about to send forth the principle of life. He did not fail to rouse me by every possible means, 'till I was convinced of the reality of what I saw and heard. I tryed to walk, but my legs were so weak, and my feet so tender, that I could no longer move. My deliverer, therefore, got me on his back, and carried me to the gondola, where I found this lady, in the greatest joy on my arrival. We were now rowed silently along the great canal, and then acrofs the lake that separates Venice from the main land. We found a coach, ready for our reception

ception on the beach, and before break of day, we got into the dominions of the Emperor. Here we stopped until I took a little rest, and had my legs wrapped in warm flannel, for they were half putrid, the fœtid muscles dropping off from the bones below.

" I now learned, for the first time, from my wife, the history of my deliverance. After they had seized us, as I have informed you, she was shut up in a convent, from which she found means, in a short time to make her escape. She immediately changed her dress, and luckily applying for informatian about me to this jailor, who had been a servant of her father's, she prevailed on him with tears, entreaties

treaties and promises, to attempt what he had so happily accomplished. The coach we found by the side of the lake was one of my own, which the jailor's son had brought from my house on the Brent.

"For such a wonderful escape from the jealous eye of a Venetian government, exclaimed Signor Tedeschi, you can never be sufficiently thankful. If the superior powers at any time interfere in the actions of men, this may be allowed one of the most surprizing instances. But let me hear, my friend, the particulars of your journey to England."

Signor Antonio resumed his narrative. "At Infpruck, that beautiful city, furrounded on every fide with mountains, I ftopped till my recovery was completed. We then purfued our journey to England, through the Tyrol. The road is along the fide of a river, which runs in a narrow valley that divides thefe immenfe ridges. I was delighted with the happy and independent appearance of the inhabitants of thefe romantic fpots. They are quite feparated from the reft of the world by nature.—The fon lives in peace where the father died of age, and he cultivates the very field which has nourifhed all his race. The profpect from this road is one of the moft romantic that can be conceived. On every

every side of it, the cliffs are covered with wood to a great height, and towards the top they are white with snow. Betwixt these mountains lies the valley I have mentioned, where we had summer in all its luxury. The poor inhabitants were spread over the plain, employed in the different offices of their agriculture. Now and then their simple cottages afforded a contrast to the rude majesty of a ruined castle, which some knight had built on a precipice, in the days of tilt and tournament. Tyrolesians, cryed I, on leaving their mountains, where I had rode several days; your situation and your poverty defend you against oppression!—Tyrolesians, you have no science; but you have inno-

innocence, you have no politics, but you have happiness.

"From these cliffs we descended into a country, where nature seems to have been at particular pains to smooth the fields, which as well as the trees, were covered with a beautiful verdure. But we saw few inhabitants of the human species, in a place so favourable for their growth. Now and then a wild beast ran growling across the road, as if displeased at our entering into a region which mankind has relinquished for his use.— I have often since that time lamented the cursed effects of tyranny and war on this pleasant country. How many voices might have praised heaven in deserts,

where

where silence and solitude at present reign, *but for* the ambition and oppression of the rulers of the earth.

"I shall say nothing of Augsburg, which is a pleasant town, where the inhabitants have painted battles, &c. on the walls of their houses that face the street.

"At Frankfort we arrived at the time of their fair, which is the greatest in the world. It was very entertaining to look at the heterogeneous multitude that were assembled on this occasion. The streets as well as the shops were laden with the productions of every part of the continent. Furs from Russia, herrings from Holland, and
ribbons

ribbons from France, served to give an idea of trade, and an appearance of the different nations.—— The Jews mixed with Chriſtians, all was in commotion, every face was full of anxiety, and every man tried to cheat his neighbour, and ſo we left Frankfort.

"At Bruſſels, through which we alſo paſſed, we found the nobility as well as the inferior ranks, more inſignificant than you can well conceive. Their whole knowledge conſiſts in a little French, and their whole ſtudy is in imitation of the follies, without the merits of that nation. I have ſeen a rough little thing they called my lady, look with the ferocity of a wild beaſt, from a ſide box in the play-houſe, on all the audience around; while she spoke aloud to an acquaintance, to demonstrate of how little consequence it was that inferior people should be disturbed. From Brussels we came by the way of Ostend to London, where we have only been a few days.

"Though I knew you was here, I was ignorant of your address, and found myself much at a loss how to discover you. What aggravated my disappointment in not being able to get any information about you, the master of the inn where we lodged, began to find that my money was exhausted, which you will not wonder at, considering the nature of our escape. This gave him a notion that we wanted to cheat

cheat him, which my imperfect way of speaking English tended to confirm.—He began to tell us that people must be paid, and at last openly insisted that I should dispose of some things to discharge his bill. For this purpose he carried me to a shop, where I have left a few miniatures of my friends, and several gold medals of my ancestors. But continued Signor Antonio, I should be glad to hear how you got to London.

"THAT I can tell you, answered Signor Tedeschi in a few words. We had a prosperous voyage to Holland, whence I came over to England with all your wealth, and what remained of my own at Venice. Yours, I have disposed in such

such a way till your arrival, as I judged most advantageous, of which I hope to be able to convince you to morrow.—But let us forget all business at present, and after I have stepped as far as the pawn broker's shop, to redeem the things you mention, we will spend the evening all together in happiness.

WITH all my heart said the lady Francisca.—The prospect of better days in a land of liberty, shall entirely banish care from my pillow to night.

CHAP.

CHAP. XVIII.

THE CHIMNEY SWEEP.—I LEAVE THE PAWN-BROKER'S SHOP, AND AM CARRIED BY A LOVER TO HIS MISTRESS.——A DISSERTATION ON VINEGAR DRINKING, AS PRACTISED BY THE LADIES IN TOWN AND COUNTRY.

THE laſt of my maſter's cuſtomer's for the night, was a chimney-ſweep about twelve years of age, who bought ſome little neceſſa-

necessaries with the profits of the day. My master observing that he had no teeth in the fore part of his jaws, asked the boy by what accident he had lost them. "By "no accident," replied the sweep, "my mother sold them when I "was young, to a dentist, who "transplanted them into the head "of an old lady of quality. But "I had the pleasure of hearing "since, that her gums, rotten with "disease and sweetmeats, did not "long retain my property, for "they fell down her throat, one "night when she was a-sleep, and "she never once awakened since that "time." "Fie upon such a shame- "ful practice," answered my mas- ter, "it is too common an enormity, "and calls aloud for the notice of
"the

"the magistrate. Though I have
"been much used to make mo-
"ney of the wretched, I swear I
"would rather beg in the streets,
"than ride in a coach by such
"means as these." "My sister,"
replied the boy, "is much worse
"off than I am, for she has had
"nothing but her naked jaws,
"since she was nine years of age.
"It is but a poor comfort to her,
"that her teeth are at court,
"while she lives at home on
"slops, without any hopes of a
"husband."

The time of my bidding farewel to the pawn-broker was now
arrived, for on shutting up his
shop, I was carried to a large
dealer in light gold.

MY

My new master was an overgrown little fellow, considerably advanced in years. He picked me out amongst a variety of Portuguese and other coins, and putting me into his pocket, walked along Fleet-street on his tiptoe, constantly comparing his own figure with those that passed us. Now reader, you must not be surprized, when I tell you, that my little master, with an immense belly, large cheeks, and a big head, drew every comparison to his own advantage; for though he was often obliged to allow, that some men were taller, or had considerably a smaller proportion of fat, yet he always discovered something agreeable in himself, that over-balanced these advantages.—

He

He was going at present on an important affair, which excited every spark of fire, that remained in his constitution. This was to visit a tailor's daughter, of whom he was much enamoured, and with whom he was on the point of being married.

When we arrived at the door of her father's house, my master examined his dress, *de capite ad calcem*, from the head to the hoof, and then anounced his presence, by a loud peal of thunder on the brass knocker at the door. It is well known in this city, that the noise of a person's approach, is in proportion to the opinion he entertains of his own importance. My master had very exalted ideas
of

of his confequence, and he had much reafon, for he had much money. His reception was equal to his expectations; Mifs Rogers meets him with much apparent joy,—the children are driven from the fire to make room for him,—Chloe, the lap-lady, is difcompofed, and Daphne, the cat, is rudely treated,—the lover is fet on the fofteft chair of the apartment, and in the warmeft corner of it. After difcuffing fome political topics, the prudent parents retire, to give room for amorous daliance. I could fee the fituation of both hearts at the fame time. The one was inflamed with a filly impotent paffion, the other was full of averfion and difguft. My mafter played the part of an old fool, and

mifs

miss that of a young hypocrite. Before parting, he gave me to the lady as a keep-sake, with a promise to bring her a poem he had just composed, which had the additional merit of being an acrostic, that he assured her limped very prettily in its chains.

He was no sooner out of the house, than she rung the bell. "Nanny," said she to the maid, on entering, "get me some soap "and water to wash away the "scum of that toad, and tell my "dear George, he may venture "up stairs."

As George was already gone away, I remained with this lady all night; for from the moment I came

I came into her possession, I was destined, for that favoured youth.

I HAD now time to take a view of my new mistress. As she was bred in the country, her face was flushed with health. Like a Grecian beauty she was rather fat than lean. Though her waist was none of the smallest it was by no means the less handsome, and by much the more desirable. With such endowments of person, I thought any female might have been well contented; but my mistress in compliance with fashion, had taken it into her head that she was by much too fat. To remedy this defect, and correct the erring hand of nature, from time to time, she took

took a draught of vinegar in private. The fluids by the power of this poison, began to move with less force in the vessels of the surface. Her appetite was weakened, and every organ of digestion lost its vigour.

Foolish maid, thought I, you wish to improve your beauty by destroying your health. Your folly is equal to your crime. The one cannot exist almost for a moment without the other. While the very purpose you try to answer will soon be for ever beyond your reach by the means you take to attain it; you are marked down in heaven as a deliberate suicide. But it is not yourself alone you destroy. One of the first commands of heaven, is to increase and multiply; to obey this command, in a short time you will be totally unfit. Sterility will remain a curse on your name. Or, if some faint being finds its way, by your means, into the precincts of day, it will have reason from disease to curse the vanity of its parent. Worse than suicide, you destroy your beauty, and poison your health, while old age advances towards you with a rapidity which nature would never have allowed!

In the morning George made his appearance, who received me from my mistress, giving his word he would never part with me, for the giver's sake, and before night, I found myself in the possession of a
sweet

sweet girl, who attended on an appendage of the court. By her I was given to one of those women, who are employed in taking care of the lovely children of the greatest King, who gave me as a plaything to the young princess.

L 4. CHAP.

queen xvi. who pressed me to appear before at the court. I have, I wis, spent a great part of the time, who are employed in taking care of the lovely children of the great elf King, who gave me as a plaything to the young prince.

CHAP.

CHAP. XIX.

THE QUEEN.---A LOVER.

MY present mistress was a mere child, though more lovely than the little god of poisoned arrows.—She was at play in a room with eight or ten of her brothers and sisters, when I entered into her service.—I wish I could give you an idea of the pleasure I felt on seeing this young family of princes and princesses, entertaining themselves with the little sports of youth, while the maxims a parent had imbibed, fell from their artless lips, in all the beauteous simplicity of nature.— It is thus the young mind should receive the principles of virtue, for as the twig is bent the tree for ever grows. The first ideas men get from education, are commonly the last they retain at the extremity of life. At any rate, they make a strong impression, which reason with difficulty is able to efface at a future period. How careful therefore ought we to be, that the first notions have their foundation in truth, how anxious to separate

right

right from wrong in the mind of the infant.

Such reflections as these occupied my attention, on seeing the mutual harmony of the royal babes. I was listening with pleasure to their little observations, which were tinged by the source from which they took their rise, and I was admiring that wisdom which could direct with so much art, the infant stream of ideas, when the queen entered the room. The little family immediately surrounded her, each telling his important story to attract her attention. Her face was expressive of the highest happiness, while her eyes feasted themselves on the innocent pratlers.— She interrested herself in their affairs, stood umpire in every matter of difference, and with the utmost judgment, commended some and reprimanded others.

Happy sovereign, you are not only exalted above all your people in dignity but in merit. You are the favourite of a nation that values itself above every other, with the disadvantage of not being even a native of it. There is no rank of life that does not admire your virtues; you have not a good subject who does not wish to imitate them.

As I had often found that the face is not a sufficient index of the state of the mind, nor the particular actions of mankind a sufficient basis for forming a just opinion of them,

them, I resolved to avail myself of my power of reading the real state of things from the characters of the brain. For this purpose I made the fullest analysis be taken of the ideas of this beloved queen; and believe me, reader, there is not one of them which would not do honour to the purest system of morality. The Tuscan philosopher never felt more pleasure in examining the appearance of the heavenly orbs, than I did at the view of such earthly perfection. The queen was so blended with the woman, that the one created love, while the other raised admiration.

I PASSED some time in this delightful service, during which period

riod I had every day more reason to admire this sovereign. Hyder Alli was the only potentate I had before visited. Though he possessed intrepidity and power, and genius, and even generosity, his mind was perpetually on the rack. He was continually forming dark designs to accomplish his bloody purposes. I have heard him cry out, " may heaven send that " glorious day, when I can wreck " my vengeance on these white " men that infest our country.— " When I can cut in pieces every " limb of theirs that has ventured " into our India. The groans of " their friends in a distant region " will be to Hyder Alli the truest " tributes of praise."

How

How different are the sentiments of Britannia's queen! she wishes well to all mankind, and that they may be happy, she points out the road of virtue in her own practice; by which alone they can attain it.

The king was so busy during my residence in these blest abodes, that I had no opportunity of seeing him. He was holding in his hands the scales in which mighty kingdoms were weighed. Almost all the nations in the earth had taken up arms against his sea surrounded land; but their impotent efforts will expose them to contempt, while Britain shall remain the admiration of future times.——Great monarch, into whatever country your free born subjects
move

move, they shall carry in their hands both victory and law!

My little mistress lost me in St. James's park, where I might have remained amongst the grass for many years, had it not been for a Westminster lover, who had reclined himself on the verdant turf to enjoy the zephyrs of noon. He sometimes thought and sometimes wrote, till he had finished the following performance, which fell from his heart with the ease of sincerity.

TO MY ANNA.

IN Temple Yard unknown in song,
  Where ne'er a rose-bud blows,
Where ne'er a zephyr moves along,
  Nor riv'let ever flows;

No shepherd here, in am'rous lays,
  Salutes the rising morn,
No landscape lost in many a maze,
  Nor dew-drop on the thorn,

But all the glory of this place,
  Is Anna! peerless maid;
And such a mind, with such a face,
  Was never sung or said.

I will not praise this maiden's eye;
  Tho' sooth to say I may—
Nor yet her lip of heavenly dye,
  Where little cupids play.

The infant spring in robes of green,
  Is not so fair as she;
Tho' fair as infant spring I ween,
  May other damsel's be;

But others cannot take a part,
  In every mourner's woe,
Nor can they boast the gentlest heart,
  In bosom white as snow.---

But I must bid all hope farewel---
  My Anna eke adieu,
For I can never, never tell,
  The half of all your due.

This young man layed hold of me with a disconsolate look,--- "Curst gold," he cries, "it is "by your pernicious influence, "that I must be for ever torn "from my Anna. Was I in pos- "session of a quantity of such "earth

"earth we had never separated
"in life, and death should
"have inclosed us in the same
"grave. But I must obey my
"destiny without murmuring. I
"must with patience behold the
"loss of, all, I fear to lose. Anna,
"in a short time, seas shall roll
"between us, and mountains shall
"rise to divide us. We shall never
"see the chearful days that our
"imaginations had formed in each
"other's company; and if ever we
"meet again, it will only be to
"notice the ravages of time on our
"decayed persons, before they
"drop into the dust, out of which
"they were originally made."

My master was going abroad in
the service of his country. I had
fre-

frequent opportunities before leaving him to see the effects of his unhappy passion. He is one of these mortals, on whom nature has bestowed too much taste and sensibility for his fortune or happiness. I shall never think of him without esteem, I shall never recollect him without sorrow.

CHAP.

CHAP. XX.

MILITARY EDUCATION.----A JEW AN HONEST MAN.

ON going home from the park, my master, who belonged to the army, met with an officer of the same regiment with himself. I soon discovered this stranger to be that soldier, whose brain my spirit had searched with
so

so much accuracy, without finding any ideas.—" How do you do Bob," said he to my mafter, " I have juft been dining with fome fine girls, and am at prefent going into the park, to fee if there are any new faces moving about. Afterwards I fhall take a turn into the city to call on fome young ladies, who I am fure are damned angry with me for not feeing them before now; and after making two or three more vifits in that quarter, I fhall return to Harley-ftreet, where a large company of us are to fpend the evening. Is not my hair damned well dreffed to day Bob? But your fervant fir." Your fervant faid my mafter, who had not before an opportunity of opening his lips. As I perceived him

very

very thoughtful after this encounter with his friend, I ordered a review to be taken of his brain at that inftant, from the hope of knowing fomething of the foldier's hiftory, which I now was anxious to learn; for like women, I have the ftrongeft defire of being acquainted with every thing, however little connection I may have with it, provided it is a fecret, and especially a fecret difficult to come at. I was not difappointed, for my mafter was really thinking of his fellow foldier and pitying him.

This youth, is the younger fon of a good family. In his early years he would learn nothing that could either be ufeful or ornamental,

mental, and he saw manhood approach, with the neceffity of doing fomething for his bread, without the knowledge of any thing that could enable him to acquire it. His friends propofed his going into the army as the only means to get rid of him, to which he was not averfe. But it was not the defire of fame, it was not the hope of diftinguifhing himfelf in the fervice of his country, that prompted him—Thefe were ideas infinitely beyond the capacity of his conception. His chief inducement was its being a genteel profeffion, which required, as he thought, no ftudy, joined to the fplendour of a red coat, which his contracted mind placed in the higheft rank of enjoyment. My reader would not credit me, if I
were

were to tell him the number of females that have fallen a prey to our soldier; for as his mind has nothing in itself that can contribute to its own entertainment, he is obliged to kill the time, as far as possible, with the pleasures of love, eating, and drinking.

WHAT a just idea, thought my master, does the history of this gentleman give of many of our military youths.—Without science, without the capacity of acquiring any, with no knowledge of war, and with no predilection for the army that reason can justify, a young man in this country is made an officer.—He gets a cockade, an epaulet, a sword, and a commission; and he never suspects that he is unfit for his business, nor does the world ever suspect it. While surgeons are appointed to examine the state of the common soldier's body, it might be equally proper to look a little into the temper of the officer's mind. This might be attended with the best effect in a nation like ours, where a mercantile spirit is so contrary to the military.—May we not account for the great success of the India Company, by the manner their officers attain a high command.—It is not because a man is of a noble family, or has a weighty purse; it is known abilities and former services that entitle him to a distinguished rank. For my part, I think, that in the same proportion as the mind is nobler than the body,

body, and in the same degree that an officer's power exceeds that of a common soldier, the qualifications of the mind should be more accurately examined than those of the body.

While my master was making these reflections, he arrived at his lodgings, where he found a friend that waited his return. "How "are you Moses," said he to the stranger, "I expected to see you "early this morning as you had "promised me." "I have been "busy" said Moses, "in endeavour"ing to get the little son of Mrs. "M. into the hospital, we shall "hear to night the effect of my ap"plication. You know he lost his "father, who was a lieutenant in

" one of his majesty's ships, by that
" dreadful hurricane in the West-
" Indies. She is an amiable discon-
" solate woman, I think no body has
" a better title than her son, and I
" shall never be happy, till I can
" render some service to the boy of
" my deceased friend. Oh! he
" was the best of men, and of all
" others I respected him the most;
" how often has he told me—I was
" born a christian, my friend, and
" you, by a like effect of chance,
" were a Jew by birth. You are
" a native of one kingdom and I
" of another. But let not distinc-
" tions, which neither of us can
" help, tend in any degree to
" weaken our friendship. We are
" connected by ties that time and
" place cannot alter—I am a man
    " as

"as well as you.—Like yourself I
"feel the emotions of humanity,
"like yourself, I wish to obey the
"precepts of morality. We do
"not owe our friendship to chance,
"it was a similarity of sentiment
"that first connected us, it is
"a similarity of sentiment that
"has confirmed the connection."
While Moses was going on in
this manner about his old friend,
with the tears starting from his
eyes, a girl from Mrs. M. came
running into the room. "Oh!
"sir, said she, addressing the Jew,
"my mistress has got Jack into
"the hospital, and desires to
"see you immediately." Without waiting to bid my master farewel, the good natured man

flew to congratulate the poor widow, on her fuccefs.

"This Jew" cried my mafter as foon as he was gone, "this Jew "might be a pattern to the beft "of us, who value ourfelves on the "name of chriftians. I know him "well, and I know there never was "a more generous foul that animat-"ed a human form. The defire "of doing good in a greater de-"gree, is his only motive for fuch "extreme application to bufinefs. "May his fcattered nation find "out fome refting place at laft, to "call by the dear appellation of "country! — May chriftians at "length forget to perfecute their "fellow mortals for a mere matter "of opinion!—When we ceafe to
"opprefs

"oppress them, they will cease to
"deserve the character of knaves;
"and by giving them the rights
"of men, we shall not only make
"them our friends, but more valu-
"able members of our society."

M 5   CHAP.

CHAP. XXI.

THE LITTLE WOMAN IN GREAT-QUEEN STREET.

BY a few common changes that perpetually happen to gold, I found myself in the poffeffion of a little man, with a great hump back,—as the poet says,

"His

"His mountain back might well be said,
"To meafure height above his head."

Nature has been very beneficent to men of this clafs, for what they want in reality, they generally make up in idea. This was the cafe, in an eminent degree, with my prefent mafter, whom the children of eighty to the children of eight, had diftinguifhed by the title of,—My Lord.

WITH this little man, I lived happily enough for fome time, and without meeting any thing remarkable, 'till one day he got himfelf dreffed much better than ufual to vifit his miftrefs, for the " crea-
" ture dared to love." He was
full

full of conceit on this occasion, although he could scarce convince himself, but he saw something on his posterior parts, which should not have been there. After a great deal of business with the looking-glass, which, I could see, sometimes conveyed a pain amidst its pleasures, he directed his course to Great-queen-street, where he was petitioned by the poor little woman, who has taken her stand at one of the ends of it. " I always " pity," said my master aloud, " I sincerely pity the blasted part " of the creation. Though I am " not so tall as a Scotchman, yet " I have reason to thank heaven, " that has made me not inferior " to other men." The word *Scotchman*, made its way to the ear of a

native

native of that country, who was dreſſed in petticoats and a bonnet. As all the other parts of the ſentence were loſt, before they reached ſuch a diſtance, the Caledonian made no doubt of its being a national reflection. He therefore approached my maſter, almoſt petrified with the ferocity of his look, and the length of his broad ſword. "Brat at you arr," ſaid he, "will you preten to caſt oot
"national reflections on oor kin-
"try. I hif a gude mind to ſwal-
"low you, gin I kent your back
"widna ſtick in my thrapple.—
"At ony rate, gin you ſpeak a-
"nither wird, I'll piſs oot your
"life, you brat at you arr." My maſter had by this time ſhut his eyes, for he could no longer bear
the

the inflamed visage of the brawny Scot, and was moving away as fast as possible, directing himself by the wall, when his head pitched into the groin of an anabaptist preacher, who had just delivered a sermon on the insufficiency, or rather sinfulness of morality. It is not for me to describe, with what sort of substance the head came into contact; it is enough to say, that it was a substance which should not have been there. To leave this matter in the dark where it was conceived; the rude meeting gave the poor preacher such exquisite pain, that he roared out with more noise than a warlike instrument. Never was there a train of more unlucky accidents; my master imagining that the sound he heard, and the shock he had received, proceeded from the Scot beginning to execute his threats, shut his eyes with more vigour, and crept along with all his might. But he had not crept far, before he slipped into one of those apertures, through which they pass coals into a cellar. He moved with much velocity in his new direction, until his back came into conjuction with the margin of the opening, and there he hung, betwixt heaven and earth, by as singular a suspension as the tomb of Mahomet. Some women that happened to be below, on seeing the descent of such a figure, which stopped up the light as it fell, were thrown into fits, and two were cured of dropsies of several months duration,

duration. In this situation all parties continued for some time, my master never doubting, for he durst not open his eyes, that he was in another world, by a blow from the Scotchman; which was not to be wondered at, considering the motion and concussions his brain had undergone. At length, he was with difficulty set at liberty by some good-natured passengers, and carried home.

This should be a lesson to every person, to learn exactly what he is himself and never to despise the little woman in Great-queen-street.

CHAP.

CHAP. XXII.

ALEXANDER, JULIUS CÆSAR, CATO, CATALINE, LORD G. G――N, VENUS, AND MINERVA.

GENTLE reader, this shall be the last chapter of my adventures, for I would not for Hyder Alli's kingdom, tell any thing that is not absolutely true, though by acting otherwise, I might imitate many grave historians, and celebrated biographers.

I AM

I AM at present safely laid up in the storehouse of a society of antiquarians, where, with medals, busts, inscriptions, and other of my learned brethren, I spend my hours in separating truth from the ashes of time. Our eyes can penetrate with the same ease the shade of antiquity, and the prejudices that surround the present day. We say, without fear of punishment, that Alexander the Great was a man, or that Julius Cæsar was a bald man. We exclaim, that the duchess of ——, is a w——e; that general ——, is neither a soldier nor a writer; and admiral ——, neither a sailor nor a fighter. But amidst such a number of both ancients and moderns, that compose our collection, I never saw but two instances of any

any interruption to our concord.

One of these was a squabble of a copper head of my Lord G—— G——, with a silver figure of Minerva.—The other was a quarrel, which a miniature face of the old lord who divorced the young lady had, with a Venus Genetrix. In order to make up matters betwixt the two last, and to enjoy a little peace at home, we placed Venus, by her own desire, beside a coronation figure of his Majesty; and, to do her justice, she has been quiet ever since.

But it is proper to inform you, reader, how I came into this society, and you will wonder,

der, when I tell you, it was by the hands of a good man, though not a rich man, who has been a governor, and a governor of a rich ifland. But what is as furprifing, this governor of a rich ifland, who is not a rich man, is a foldier, and yet a fcholar; for, like Fabricus, he defpifes wealth, while, like George the Third, he values learning. This gentleman happening to fee me, refolved to purchafe me of my crooked mafter, for, I think, I have before obferved, that gold never before improved itfelf to the degree that I have done.

In this place, I am like to pafs a number of happy years, amongft many of the great men of
anti-

antiquity. Cato gave us a long oration to day againſt the vices of the age, and concluded it with reprimanding Cataline, who had ventured to commend the burning of the city. He ſpoke with much ſeverity againſt corruption, from which he naturally paſſed to cenſure the Britiſh parliament. Some of the members, I think, he commended for diſintereſtedneſs; and, amongſt others, he did not forget a Mr. D——r, for whom he has a particular friendſhip.

* * * * * * * * *

I HAVE great reaſon, reader, to make an apology for the number of my chapters, which number, I think, contains in itſelf no myſtic property that can affect

fect the soul's salvation; I am ashamed to own, that as far as I know, it has even no power in the cure of bodily disease. In short, I have no apology to make for the choice of twenty-two, for it is neither the number prefered by Homer, Virgil, nor Milton.

After such a candid confession, I must bid you, gentle reader, farewel. If you have any brains, which suppofition, take my word, whatever yourself may think, is a thousand to one against the brains, you must be improved by my adventures; which will stand you in stead of experience, and give you some knowledge of mankind, without impairing the good qualities of your heart.

THE END.

www.ingramcontent.com/pod-product-compliance
Lightning Source LLC
Chambersburg PA
CBHW032118230426
43672CB00009B/1781